3Ninety3

A journey to connect with Christlikeness

FOURTH SEAT
COLLECTIVE
——— PUBLISHING ———

Table of Contents

Putting on Christ'...is not one among
many jobs a Christian has to do;
and it is not a sort of special
exercise for the top class.
It is the whole of Christianity.
Christianity offers nothing else at all.

*-C.S. **Lewis**, Mere Christianity*

Welcome to the 3Ninety3 Journey!

What exactly is 3Ninety3? In the simplest of terms, 3Ninety3 is a journey to connect with Christlikeness.

What is our goal? This is a journey to begin the process of spiritual formation. We have all been through some type of spiritual formation, even if we don't realize it. Dallas Willard said, "Everyone gets a spiritual formation. It's like education. Everyone gets an education; it's just a matter of which one you get."[1] God's intention is for each of us to be conformed to the image of Christ and eventually transformed into a completely new creation. Just like his first disciples, our goal is to walk so closely with Jesus that we too can hear his voice and discern his voice, eventually living in the confidence of knowing what he would do if he were in our place at any given moment.

How are we going to do it? We will do this through a three-day launch, followed by a ninety-day personal walk with Jesus, and culminated with a three-day landing. Each step plays a key role in our spiritual development.

---

[1] "The Making of the Christian." *ChristianityToday.com,* 16 Sept. 2005, https://www.christianitytoday.com/ct/2005/october/9.42.html.

What do I need to bring to this journey?

Commitment. Jesus, unlike your mother, will not drag you along this path kicking and screaming. This journey will only take you as far as your commitment is firm.

Respect. we are all different and we all have different ways of expressing our thoughts. Refrain from being judgmental of those in your community, let everyone know they are loved and welcome.

Openness. in our journey we do not pretend to have a corner on the Jesus Market. During the launch and landing you will hear quotes from a deep well of Christian experience.

Confidentiality. No one likes a gossip, except a gossip. During our journey we will form a community and the bedrock of that community is confidentiality. Don't allow your tongue to damage the work that the Holy Spirit is doing.

Three Day Launch

What is a three-day launch? It would be wise to envision the first three-day launch as an orientation of sorts. During this time together we will define a clear direction we will be using as our true north, we will work to clarify and simplify what Jesus expects from his followers. As finite humans we all suffer from a tendency to drift, for that reason it will be important to take notes and revisit the talks we will share during these days to assure that you remain on the right path. We will also work to build a community of like-minded spiritual travelers; this community will provide support during the crucial Ninety-day walk of your journey with Jesus.

Session 1: Who is God?

Love Letter To My Beloved Child

- You may not know me, but I have known you since your very beginning—*Ps. 139:1*
  I am familiar with all your ways—*Ps. 139:3*
  Even the very hairs on your head are numbered
  — *Matt. 10:29-31*
  For you were made in my image—*Gen. 1:27*
  In me you live and move and have your being—*Acts 17:28*

  For you are my offspring—*Acts 17:28*
  I knew you even before you were conceived—*Jer. 1:4-5*
- I chose you when I planned creation—*Eph. 1:11-12*
  You were not a mistake, for all your days are written in my book—*Ps. 139:15-16*
  You are fearfully and wonderfully made—*Ps. 139:14*

  I knit you together in your mother's womb—*Ps. 139:13*
  I have been misrepresented by those who don't know me
  —*John 8:41-44*
- I am not distant and angry, but am the complete expression of love—*1 John 4:16*
  And it is my desire to lavish my love on you—*1 John 3:1*

  I love you more than your earthly parent ever could—*Matt. 7:11*

  For I am the perfect Parent—*Matt. 5:48*
  Every good gift that you receive comes from my hand—*James 1:17*
  For I am your provider and I will meet all your needs —*Matt. 6:31-33*
  My plan for your future has always been filled with hope—*Jer. 29:11*
  Because I love you with an everlasting love—*Jer. 31:3*

  My thoughts toward you are countless as the sand on the seashore—*Ps. 139:17-18*
  And I rejoice over you with singing—*Zeph. 3:17*
  I will never stop doing good to you—*Jer. 32:40*
  For you are my treasure child—*Ex. 19:5*

I desire to establish you with all my heart and all my soul—*Jer. 32:41*
And I want to show you great and marvelous things—*Jer. 33:3*
⌐ If you seek me with all your heart, you will find me—*Deut. 4:29*
Delight in me, and I will give you the desires of your heart
—*Ps. 37:4*
For it is I who gave you those desires—*Phil. 2:13*
I am able to do more for you than you could possibly imagine
—*Eph. 3:20*

For I am your greatest encourager—*2 Thes. 2:16-17*
I am also the Parent who comforts you in all your troubles
—*2 Cor. 1:3-4*
When you are brokenhearted, I am close to you—*Ps. 34:18*
As a shepherd carries a lamb, I have carried you close to my
heart—*Isa. 40:11*
⌐ One day, I will wipe away every tear from your eyes—*Rev. 21:3-4*

And I will take away all the pain you have suffered on this
earth—*Rev. 21:3-4*
I am your Beloved, and I love you even as I love Jesus—*John 17:23*
⌐ For in Jesus, my love for you is revealed—*John 17:26* Jesus is
the exact representation of my being—*Heb. 1:3*
Jesus came to demonstrate that I am for you, not against you
—*Rom. 8:31*

If you are friends with Jesus, you are friends with me
—*1 John 2:23*
And nothing will ever separate you from my love—*Rom. 8:38-39*
Come to me, and I'll throw the biggest party heaven or earth has
ever seen—*Luke 15:7*[2]

---

[2] "Love Letter to My Beloved Child." Introducing the Cycle of Grace,
20 Sep, 2019, Renovaré Institute. Class handout.

Notes:

Notes:

Session 2: Who Do You Say I Am?

Colossians 3:1-17 (NLT)

1 Since you have been raised to new life with Christ, set your sights on the realities of heaven, where Christ sits in the place of honor at God's right hand. 2 Think about the things of heaven, not the things of earth. 3 For you died to this life, and your real life is hidden with Christ in God. 4 And when Christ, who is your life, is revealed to the whole world, you will share in all his glory. 5 So put to death the sinful, earthly things lurking within you. Have nothing to do with sexual immorality, impurity, lust, and evil desires. Don't be greedy, for a greedy person is an idolater, worshiping the things of this world. 6 Because of these sins, the anger of God is coming. 7 You used to do these things when your life was still part of this world.8 But now is the time to get rid of anger, rage, malicious behavior, slander, and dirty language. 9 Don't lie to each other, for you have stripped off your old sinful nature and all its wicked deeds.10 Put on your new nature, and be renewed as you learn to know your Creator and become like him.11 In this new life, it doesn't matter if you are a Jew or a Gentile, circumcised or uncircumcised, barbaric, uncivilized, slave, or free. Christ is all that matters, and he lives in all of us. 12 Since God chose you to be the holy people he loves, you must clothe yourselves with tenderhearted mercy, kindness, humility, gentleness, and patience. 13 Make allowance for each other's faults, and forgive anyone who offends you. Remember, the Lord forgave you, so you must forgive others. 14 Above all, clothe yourselves with love, which binds us all together in perfect harmony. 15 And let the peace that comes from Christ rule in your hearts. For as members of one body you are called to live in peace. And always be thankful. 16 Let the message about Christ, in all its richness, fill your lives. Teach and counsel each other with all the wisdom he gives. Sing psalms and hymns and spiritual songs to God with thankful hearts. 17 And whatever you do or say, do it as a representative of the Lord Jesus, giving thanks through him to God the Father.

Notes:

- If I don't see it in Jesus, I can't attribute it to God.
- God loves us as we are, not as we should be. Psalms give us permission to not be perfect.
- Read Sermon on the Mount through the lens of the fact that Jesus already came to establish his realm. It is not "yonder". We were created for it!
- The glory of God is man <u>fully</u> <u>alive.</u>

Notes:

Session 3: My Yoke is Easy

What does a good listener do?

1. Slow down. *Hurry is the enemy!*
2. Listen until the end. *Don't assume*
3. Consider the whole message that is being communicated. *Don't cherry pick*
4. Ask questions. (Turn it around and Chew on it.)
5. Write down what you are hearing.
6. If one knows, really knows the person they are listening to, one can infer meaning. (Non-verbal's). What's being said without being said? How does this sound in light of what I know to be true of the person saying it? Note: Many Christians skip to inferring meaning way too quickly, because they are in a hurry and are unwilling to slow down to hear what is truly being said.

Paper is to write down what we need to remember. Brains are to think. Einstein

Notes: Hearing

- When life squeezes us, all that comes out is what is inside us. It should be Jesus.
- Spiritual formation was started John 2:5 by Mary. Discipleship.
- The only way to change bad habits is to replace them with other habits.
- "Hear" is the most important command. God is always talking. Do we translate it to what we want?
- God communicates through the sacraments.
- Marriage is the first thing God did with people. First message to us.
- 1 Samuel 3:1-10 "Speak, your servant is listening."
- asking - Teach us to pray. Lord's Prayer 3x a day. Pray like you eat dark chocolate.
- The Psalms are Jesus' prayer book.

- Notes: <u>wilderness</u>

mozart said music is not in the notes but in the silence inbetween. Focused silence.

- <u>Self Denial</u> - Fasting (beyond food)
Christ-centered = self denying

- <u>Sabbath</u> - Made for man. Man needs Sabbath. Take the time. Rest!
If you're too busy to do this, you're too busy.

- <u>Generosity</u> - the same measure you use, it will come back to you. Not about $. merciful, don't judge or condemn. Can't give what you don't have.

- <u>Beholding</u> - long and loving look. Seeing God in his creation, art, + others.

22

Session 4: Trust the Process

Patient Trust

Above all, trust in the slow work of God.

*We are quite naturally impatient in everything
to reach the end without delay.*

*We should like to skip the
intermediate stages.*

*We are impatient of being on the way to
something unknown, something new.*

And yet it is the law of all progress

*that it is made by passing through some
stages of instability— and that it may take
a very long time.*

*And so I think it is with you; your ideas mature
gradually—let them grow, let them shape
themselves, without undue haste.*

Don't try to force them on,

as though you could be today what time

*(that is to say, grace and circumstances
acting on your own good will)
will make of you tomorrow.*

*Only God could say what this new spirit
gradually forming within you will be. Give Our
Lord the benefit of believing that his hand
is leading you,*

*and accept the anxiety of feeling yourself in
suspense and incomplete.*
—Pierre Teilhard de Chardin[3]

---

[3] Harter, Michael, SJ, *Hears on Fire: Praying with Jesuits,* Loyola Press

Notes:

Notes:

Ninety-Day Walk with Jesus

What is the Ninety-day personal walk with Jesus? This is a time dedicated to leaning heavily into your relationship with Jesus. It will comprise of approximately 9 minutes of daily reading, as well as 3 scheduled pauses each day that last at least 3 minutes each. To maximize this part of your journey you will need to have a clear vision of what Jesus is offering you, make a commitment and stick to it, and trust the process that Jesus laid down for his disciples, even if you cannot see any results. Spiritual formation is not unlike physical formation. When exercising your body a common refrain is intensity plus consistency produce results, you don't go from the couch to the gym one day and the Olympic Games the next.

During this daily walk remember *LISTEN* and *SILENT* are made up of the same letters, take some time in silence to listen to the Holy Spirit.

Guide to the Ninety
A personal walk with Jesus

The Lords' Prayer
Mt 6: 9-13 (KJV)

Our Father which art in heaven, *Look up!*
Hallowed be thy name.

Thy kingdom come,
Thy will be done in earth,
as it is in heaven.

Give us this day our daily bread.

And forgive us our debts,
as we forgive our debtors.

And lead us not into temptation,
but deliver us from evil:
For thine is the kingdom,
and the power,
and the glory, forever.

Amen.

Day 1

Slowly Read: Matthew 1

Questions for Reflection:

Can you notice what Jesus was saying to those he spoke to when it was written?

Which word stood out to you?

Which person or persons stood out to you?

What encouraged you?

What convicted you?

What is the Holy Spirit saying to you through this text?

Pause to pray these into your life:

Pray the Lords' Prayer
Mt 6: 9-13 (KJV)

Our Father which art in heaven, Hallowed be thy name.
Thy kingdom come, Thy will be done in earth,
as it is in heaven.
Give us this day our daily bread.
And forgive us our debts, as we forgive our debtors.
And lead us not into temptation, but deliver us from evil:
For thine is the kingdom, and the power,
and the glory, forever.
Amen.

Psalm for Prayer: Psalm 1

Going Deeper:

- Listen Long and Listen Hard. Lean into what the Lord is saying to you.
- Write it down. If the God of the Universe speaks to you, you might want to write it down.
- Hold it, turn it, and chew it.
- Act on it. Celebrate, Repent, Change.
- Share it.

Notes:

Day 2

Slowly Read: Matthew 2

Questions for Reflection:

Can you notice what Jesus was saying to those he spoke to when it was written?

Which word stood out to you?

Which person or persons stood out to you?

What encouraged you?

What convicted you?

What is the Holy Spirit saying to you through this text?

Pause to pray these into your life:

Psalm for Prayer: Psalm 2

Going Deeper:

- Listen Long and Listen Hard. Lean into what the Lord is saying to you.
- Write it down. If the God of the Universe speaks to you, you might want to write it down.
- Hold it, turn it, and chew it.
- Act on it. Celebrate, Repent, Change.
- Share it.

Notes:

Day 3

Slowly Read: Matthew 3

Questions for Reflection:

Can you notice what Jesus was saying to those he spoke to when it was written?

Which word stood out to you?

Which person or persons stood out to you?

What encouraged you?

What convicted you?

What is the Holy Spirit saying to you through this text?

Pause to pray these into your life:

Pray the Lords' Prayer
Mt 6: 9-13 (KJV)

Our Father which art in heaven, Hallowed be thy name.
Thy kingdom come, Thy will be done in earth,
as it is in heaven.
Give us this day our daily bread.
And forgive us our debts, as we forgive our debtors.
And lead us not into temptation, but deliver us from evil:
For thine is the kingdom, and the power,
and the glory, forever.
Amen.

Psalm for Prayer: Psalm 3

Going Deeper:

- Listen Long and Listen Hard. Lean into what the Lord is saying to you.
- Write it down. If the God of the Universe speaks to you, you might want to write it down.
- Hold it, turn it, and chew it.
- Act on it. Celebrate, Repent, Change.
- Share it.

Notes:

Day 4

Slowly Read: Matthew 4

Questions for Reflection:

Can you notice what Jesus was saying to those he spoke to when it was written?

Which word stood out to you?

Which person or persons stood out to you?

What encouraged you?

What convicted you?

What is the Holy Spirit saying to you through this text?

Pause to pray these into your life:

Pray the Lords' Prayer
Mt 6: 9-13 (KJV)

Our Father which art in heaven, Hallowed be thy name.
Thy kingdom come, Thy will be done in earth,
as it is in heaven.
Give us this day our daily bread.
And forgive us our debts, as we forgive our debtors.
And lead us not into temptation, but deliver us from evil:
For thine is the kingdom, and the power,
and the glory, forever.
Amen.

Psalm for Prayer: Psalm 4

Going Deeper:

- Listen Long and Listen Hard. Lean into what the Lord is saying to you.
- Write it down. If the God of the Universe speaks to you, you might want to write it down.
- Hold it, turn it, and chew it.
- Act on it. Celebrate, Repent, Change.
- Share it.

Notes:

Day 5

Slowly Read: Matthew 5

Questions for Reflection:

Can you notice what Jesus was saying to those he spoke to when it was written?

Which word stood out to you?

Which person or persons stood out to you?

What encouraged you?

What convicted you?

What is the Holy Spirit saying to you through this text?

Pause to pray these into your life:

Pray the Lords' Prayer
Mt 6: 9-13 (KJV)

Our Father which art in heaven, Hallowed be thy name.
Thy kingdom come, Thy will be done in earth,
as it is in heaven.
Give us this day our daily bread.
And forgive us our debts, as we forgive our debtors.
And lead us not into temptation, but deliver us from evil:
For thine is the kingdom, and the power,
and the glory, forever.
Amen.

Psalm for Prayer: Psalm 5

Going Deeper:

- Listen Long and Listen Hard. Lean into what the Lord is saying to you.
- Write it down. If the God of the Universe speaks to you, you might want to write it down.
- Hold it, turn it, and chew it.
- Act on it. Celebrate, Repent, Change.
- Share it.

Notes:

Day 6

Slowly Read: Matthew 6

Questions for Reflection:

Can you notice what Jesus was saying to those he spoke to when it was written?

Which word stood out to you?

Which person or persons stood out to you?

What encouraged you?

What convicted you?

What is the Holy Spirit saying to you through this text?

Pause to pray these into your life:

Pray the Lords' Prayer
Mt 6: 9-13 (KJV)

Our Father which art in heaven, Hallowed be thy name.
Thy kingdom come, Thy will be done in earth,
as it is in heaven.
Give us this day our daily bread.
And forgive us our debts, as we forgive our debtors.
And lead us not into temptation, but deliver us from evil:
For thine is the kingdom, and the power,
and the glory, forever.
Amen.

Psalm for Prayer: Psalm 6

Going Deeper:

- Listen Long and Listen Hard. Lean into what the Lord is saying to you.
- Write it down. If the God of the Universe speaks to you, you might want to write it down.
- Hold it, turn it, and chew it.
- Act on it. Celebrate, Repent, Change.
- Share it.

Notes:

Day 7

Slowly Read: Matthew 7

Questions for Reflection:

Can you notice what Jesus was saying to those he spoke to when it was written?

Which word stood out to you?

Which person or persons stood out to you?

What encouraged you?

What convicted you?

What is the Holy Spirit saying to you through this text?

Pause to pray these into your life:

Pray the Lords' Prayer
Mt 6: 9-13 (KJV)

Our Father which art in heaven, Hallowed be thy name.
Thy kingdom come, Thy will be done in earth,
as it is in heaven.
Give us this day our daily bread.
And forgive us our debts, as we forgive our debtors.
And lead us not into temptation, but deliver us from evil:
For thine is the kingdom, and the power,
and the glory, forever.
Amen.

Psalm for Prayer: Psalm 7

Going Deeper:

- Listen Long and Listen Hard. Lean into what the Lord is saying to you.
- Write it down. If the God of the Universe speaks to you, you might want to write it down.
- Hold it, turn it, and chew it.
- Act on it. Celebrate, Repent, Change.
- Share it.

Notes:

Day 8

Slowly Read: Matthew 8

Questions for Reflection:

Can you notice what Jesus was saying to those he spoke to when it was written?

Which word stood out to you?

Which person or persons stood out to you?

What encouraged you?

What convicted you?

What is the Holy Spirit saying to you through this text?

Pause to pray these into your life:

Pray the Lords' Prayer
Mt 6: 9-13 (KJV)

Our Father which art in heaven, Hallowed be thy name.
Thy kingdom come, Thy will be done in earth,
as it is in heaven.
Give us this day our daily bread.
And forgive us our debts, as we forgive our debtors.
And lead us not into temptation, but deliver us from evil:
For thine is the kingdom, and the power,
and the glory, forever.
Amen.

Psalm for Prayer: Psalm 8

Going Deeper:

- Listen Long and Listen Hard. Lean into what the Lord is saying to you.
- Write it down. If the God of the Universe speaks to you, you might want to write it down.
- Hold it, turn it, and chew it.
- Act on it. Celebrate, Repent, Change.
- Share it.

Notes:

Day 9

Slowly Read: Matthew 9

Questions for Reflection:

Can you notice what Jesus was saying to those he spoke to when it was written?

Which word stood out to you?

Which person or persons stood out to you?

What encouraged you?

What convicted you?

What is the Holy Spirit saying to you through this text?

Pause to pray these into your life:

Pray the Lords' Prayer
Mt 6: 9-13 (KJV)

Our Father which art in heaven, Hallowed be thy name.
Thy kingdom come, Thy will be done in earth,
as it is in heaven.
Give us this day our daily bread.
And forgive us our debts, as we forgive our debtors.
And lead us not into temptation, but deliver us from evil:
For thine is the kingdom, and the power,
and the glory, forever.
Amen.

Psalm for Prayer: Psalm 9

Going Deeper:

- Listen Long and Listen Hard. Lean into what the Lord is saying to you.
- Write it down. If the God of the Universe speaks to you, you might want to write it down.
- Hold it, turn it, and chew it.
- Act on it. Celebrate, Repent, Change.
- Share it.

Notes:

Day 10

Slowly Read: Matthew 10

Questions for Reflection:

Can you notice what Jesus was saying to those he spoke to when it was written?

Which word stood out to you?

Which person or persons stood out to you?

What encouraged you?

What convicted you?

What is the Holy Spirit saying to you through this text?

Pause to pray these into your life:

Pray the Lords' Prayer
Mt 6: 9-13 (KJV)

*Our Father which art in heaven, Hallowed be thy name.
Thy kingdom come, Thy will be done in earth,
as it is in heaven.
Give us this day our daily bread.
And forgive us our debts, as we forgive our debtors.
And lead us not into temptation, but deliver us from evil:
For thine is the kingdom, and the power,
and the glory, forever.
Amen.*

Psalm for Prayer: Psalm 10

Going Deeper:

- Listen Long and Listen Hard. Lean into what the Lord is saying to you.
- Write it down. If the God of the Universe speaks to you, you might want to write it down.
- Hold it, turn it, and chew it.
- Act on it. Celebrate, Repent, Change.
- Share it.

Notes:

Day 11

Slowly Read: Matthew 11

Questions for Reflection:

Can you notice what Jesus was saying to those he spoke to when it was written?

Which word stood out to you?

Which person or persons stood out to you?

What encouraged you?

What convicted you?

What is the Holy Spirit saying to you through this text?

Pause to pray these into your life:

Pray the Lords' Prayer
Mt 6: 9-13 (KJV)

Our Father which art in heaven, Hallowed be thy name.
Thy kingdom come, Thy will be done in earth,
as it is in heaven.
Give us this day our daily bread.
And forgive us our debts, as we forgive our debtors.
And lead us not into temptation, but deliver us from evil:
For thine is the kingdom, and the power,
and the glory, forever.
Amen.

Psalm for Prayer: Psalm 11

Going Deeper:

- Listen Long and Listen Hard. Lean into what the Lord is saying to you.
- Write it down. If the God of the Universe speaks to you, you might want to write it down.
- Hold it, turn it, and chew it.
- Act on it. Celebrate, Repent, Change.
- Share it.

Notes:

Day 12

Slowly Read: Matthew 12

Questions for Reflection:

Can you notice what Jesus was saying to those he spoke to when it was written?

Which word stood out to you?

Which person or persons stood out to you?

What encouraged you?

What convicted you?

What is the Holy Spirit saying to you through this text?

Pause to pray these into your life:

Pray the Lords' Prayer
Mt 6: 9-13 (KJV)

Our Father which art in heaven, Hallowed be thy name.
Thy kingdom come, Thy will be done in earth,
as it is in heaven.
Give us this day our daily bread.
And forgive us our debts, as we forgive our debtors.
And lead us not into temptation, but deliver us from evil:
For thine is the kingdom, and the power,
and the glory, forever.
Amen.

Psalm for Prayer: Psalm 12

Going Deeper:

- Listen Long and Listen Hard. Lean into what the Lord is saying to you.
- Write it down. If the God of the Universe speaks to you, you might want to write it down.
- Hold it, turn it, and chew it.
- Act on it. Celebrate, Repent, Change.
- Share it.

Notes:

Day 13

Slowly Read: Matthew 13

Questions for Reflection:

Can you notice what Jesus was saying to those he spoke to when it was written?

Which word stood out to you?

Which person or persons stood out to you?

What encouraged you?

What convicted you?

What is the Holy Spirit saying to you through this text?

Pause to pray these into your life:

Pray the Lords' Prayer
Mt 6: 9-13 (KJV)

Our Father which art in heaven, Hallowed be thy name.
Thy kingdom come, Thy will be done in earth,
as it is in heaven.
Give us this day our daily bread.
And forgive us our debts, as we forgive our debtors.
And lead us not into temptation, but deliver us from evil:
For thine is the kingdom, and the power,
and the glory, forever.
Amen.

Psalm for Prayer: Psalm 13

Going Deeper:

- Listen Long and Listen Hard. Lean into what the Lord is saying to you.
- Write it down. If the God of the Universe speaks to you, you might want to write it down.
- Hold it, turn it, and chew it.
- Act on it. Celebrate, Repent, Change.
- Share it.

Notes:

Day 14

Slowly Read: Matthew 14

Questions for Reflection:

Can you notice what Jesus was saying to those he spoke to when it was written?

Which word stood out to you?

Which person or persons stood out to you?

What encouraged you?

What convicted you?

What is the Holy Spirit saying to you through this text?

Pause to pray these into your life:

Pray the Lords' Prayer
Mt 6: 9-13 (KJV)

Our Father which art in heaven, Hallowed be thy name.
Thy kingdom come, Thy will be done in earth,
as it is in heaven.
Give us this day our daily bread.
And forgive us our debts, as we forgive our debtors.
And lead us not into temptation, but deliver us from evil:
For thine is the kingdom, and the power,
and the glory, forever.
Amen.

Psalm for Prayer: Psalm 14

Going Deeper:

- Listen Long and Listen Hard. Lean into what the Lord is saying to you.
- Write it down. If the God of the Universe speaks to you, you might want to write it down.
- Hold it, turn it, and chew it.
- Act on it. Celebrate, Repent, Change.
- Share it.

Notes:

Day 15

Slowly Read: Matthew 15

Questions for Reflection:

Can you notice what Jesus was saying to those he spoke to when it was written?

Which word stood out to you?

Which person or persons stood out to you?

What encouraged you?

What convicted you?

What is the Holy Spirit saying to you through this text?

Pause to pray these into your life:

Pray the Lords' Prayer
Mt 6: 9-13 (KJV)

Our Father which art in heaven, Hallowed be thy name.
Thy kingdom come, Thy will be done in earth,
as it is in heaven.
Give us this day our daily bread.
And forgive us our debts, as we forgive our debtors.
And lead us not into temptation, but deliver us from evil:
For thine is the kingdom, and the power,
and the glory, forever.
Amen.

Psalm for Prayer: Psalm 15

Going Deeper:

- Listen Long and Listen Hard. Lean into what the Lord is saying to you.
- Write it down. If the God of the Universe speaks to you, you might want to write it down.
- Hold it, turn it, and chew it.
- Act on it. Celebrate, Repent, Change.
- Share it.

Notes:

Day 16

Slowly Read: Matthew 16

Questions for Reflection:

Can you notice what Jesus was saying to those he spoke to when it was written?

Which word stood out to you?

Which person or persons stood out to you?

What encouraged you?

What convicted you?

What is the Holy Spirit saying to you through this text?

Pause to pray these into your life:

Pray the Lords' Prayer
Mt 6: 9-13 (KJV)

Our Father which art in heaven, Hallowed be thy name.
Thy kingdom come, Thy will be done in earth,
as it is in heaven.
Give us this day our daily bread.
And forgive us our debts, as we forgive our debtors.
And lead us not into temptation, but deliver us from evil:
For thine is the kingdom, and the power,
and the glory, forever.
Amen.

Psalm for Prayer: Psalm 16

Going Deeper:

- Listen Long and Listen Hard. Lean into what the Lord is saying to you.
- Write it down. If the God of the Universe speaks to you, you might want to write it down.
- Hold it, turn it, and chew it.
- Act on it. Celebrate, Repent, Change.
- Share it.

Notes:

Day 17

Slowly Read: Matthew 17

Questions for Reflection:

Can you notice what Jesus was saying to those he spoke to when it was written?

Which word stood out to you?

Which person or persons stood out to you?

What encouraged you?

What convicted you?

What is the Holy Spirit saying to you through this text?

Pause to pray these into your life:

Pray the Lords' Prayer
Mt 6: 9-13 (KJV)

Our Father which art in heaven, Hallowed be thy name.
Thy kingdom come, Thy will be done in earth,
as it is in heaven.
Give us this day our daily bread.
And forgive us our debts, as we forgive our debtors.
And lead us not into temptation, but deliver us from evil:
For thine is the kingdom, and the power,
and the glory, forever.
Amen.

Psalm for Prayer: Psalm 17

Going Deeper:

- Listen Long and Listen Hard. Lean into what the Lord is saying to you.
- Write it down. If the God of the Universe speaks to you, you might want to write it down.
- Hold it, turn it, and chew it.
- Act on it. Celebrate, Repent, Change.
- Share it.

Notes:

Day 18

Slowly Read: Matthew 18

Questions for Reflection:

Can you notice what Jesus was saying to those he spoke to when it was written?

Which word stood out to you?

Which person or persons stood out to you?

What encouraged you?

What convicted you?

What is the Holy Spirit saying to you through this text?

Pause to pray these into your life:

Pray the Lords' Prayer
Mt 6: 9-13 (KJV)

Our Father which art in heaven, Hallowed be thy name.
Thy kingdom come, Thy will be done in earth,
as it is in heaven.
Give us this day our daily bread.
And forgive us our debts, as we forgive our debtors.
And lead us not into temptation, but deliver us from evil:
For thine is the kingdom, and the power,
and the glory, forever.
Amen.

Psalm for Prayer: Psalm 18

Going Deeper:

- Listen Long and Listen Hard. Lean into what the Lord is saying to you.
- Write it down. If the God of the Universe speaks to you, you might want to write it down.
- Hold it, turn it, and chew it.
- Act on it. Celebrate, Repent, Change.
- Share it.

Notes:

Day 19

Slowly Read: Matthew 19

Questions for Reflection:

Can you notice what Jesus was saying to those he spoke to when it was written?

Which word stood out to you?

Which person or persons stood out to you?

What encouraged you?

What convicted you?

What is the Holy Spirit saying to you through this text?

Pause to pray these into your life:

Pray the Lords' Prayer
Mt 6: 9-13 (KJV)

Our Father which art in heaven, Hallowed be thy name.
Thy kingdom come, Thy will be done in earth,
as it is in heaven.
Give us this day our daily bread.
And forgive us our debts, as we forgive our debtors.
And lead us not into temptation, but deliver us from evil:
For thine is the kingdom, and the power,
and the glory, forever.
Amen.

Psalm for Prayer: Psalm 19

Going Deeper:

- Listen Long and Listen Hard. Lean into what the Lord is saying to you.
- Write it down. If the God of the Universe speaks to you, you might want to write it down.
- Hold it, turn it, and chew it.
- Act on it. Celebrate, Repent, Change.
- Share it.

Notes:

Day 20

Slowly Read: Matthew 20

Questions for Reflection:

Can you notice what Jesus was saying to those he spoke to when it was written?

Which word stood out to you?

Which person or persons stood out to you?

What encouraged you?

What convicted you?

What is the Holy Spirit saying to you through this text?

Pause to pray these into your life:

Pray the Lords' Prayer
Mt 6: 9-13 (KJV)

Our Father which art in heaven, Hallowed be thy name.
Thy kingdom come, Thy will be done in earth,
as it is in heaven.
Give us this day our daily bread.
And forgive us our debts, as we forgive our debtors.
And lead us not into temptation, but deliver us from evil:
For thine is the kingdom, and the power,
and the glory, forever.
Amen.

Psalm for Prayer: Psalm 20

Going Deeper:

- Listen Long and Listen Hard. Lean into what the Lord is saying to you.
- Write it down. If the God of the Universe speaks to you, you might want to write it down.
- Hold it, turn it, and chew it.
- Act on it. Celebrate, Repent, Change.
- Share it.

Notes:

Day 21

Slowly Read: Matthew 21

Questions for Reflection:

Can you notice what Jesus was saying to those he spoke to when it was written?

Which word stood out to you?

Which person or persons stood out to you?

What encouraged you?

What convicted you?

What is the Holy Spirit saying to you through this text?

Pause to pray these into your life:

Pray the Lords' Prayer
Mt 6: 9-13 (KJV)

*Our Father which art in heaven, Hallowed be thy name.
Thy kingdom come, Thy will be done in earth,
as it is in heaven.
Give us this day our daily bread.
And forgive us our debts, as we forgive our debtors.
And lead us not into temptation, but deliver us from evil:
For thine is the kingdom, and the power,
and the glory, forever.
Amen.*

Psalm for Prayer: Psalm 21

Going Deeper:

- Listen Long and Listen Hard. Lean into what the Lord is saying to you.
- Write it down. If the God of the Universe speaks to you, you might want to write it down.
- Hold it, turn it, and chew it.
- Act on it. Celebrate, Repent, Change.
- Share it.

Notes:

Day 22

Slowly Read: Matthew 22

Questions for Reflection:

Can you notice what Jesus was saying to those he spoke to when it was written?

Which word stood out to you?

Which person or persons stood out to you?

What encouraged you?

What convicted you?

What is the Holy Spirit saying to you through this text?

Pause to pray these into your life:

Pray the Lords' Prayer
Mt 6: 9-13 (KJV)

Our Father which art in heaven, Hallowed be thy name.
Thy kingdom come, Thy will be done in earth,
as it is in heaven.
Give us this day our daily bread.
And forgive us our debts, as we forgive our debtors.
And lead us not into temptation, but deliver us from evil:
For thine is the kingdom, and the power,
and the glory, forever.
Amen.

Psalm for Prayer: Psalm 22

Going Deeper:

- Listen Long and Listen Hard. Lean into what the Lord is saying to you.
- Write it down. If the God of the Universe speaks to you, you might want to write it down.
- Hold it, turn it, and chew it.
- Act on it. Celebrate, Repent, Change.
- Share it.

Notes:

Day 23

Slowly Read: Matthew 23

Questions for Reflection:

Can you notice what Jesus was saying to those he spoke to when it was written?

Which word stood out to you?

Which person or persons stood out to you?

What encouraged you?

What convicted you?

What is the Holy Spirit saying to you through this text?

Pause to pray these into your life:

Pray the Lords' Prayer
Mt 6: 9-13 (KJV)

Our Father which art in heaven, Hallowed be thy name.
Thy kingdom come, Thy will be done in earth,
as it is in heaven.
Give us this day our daily bread.
And forgive us our debts, as we forgive our debtors.
And lead us not into temptation, but deliver us from evil:
For thine is the kingdom, and the power,
and the glory, forever.
Amen.

Psalm for Prayer: Psalm 23

Going Deeper:

- Listen Long and Listen Hard. Lean into what the Lord is saying to you.
- Write it down. If the God of the Universe speaks to you, you might want to write it down.
- Hold it, turn it, and chew it.
- Act on it. Celebrate, Repent, Change.
- Share it.

Notes:

Day 24

Slowly Read: Matthew 24

Questions for Reflection:

Can you notice what Jesus was saying to those he spoke to when it was written?

Which word stood out to you?

Which person or persons stood out to you?

What encouraged you?

What convicted you?

What is the Holy Spirit saying to you through this text?

Pause to pray these into your life:

Pray the Lords' Prayer
Mt 6: 9-13 (KJV)

Our Father which art in heaven, Hallowed be thy name.
Thy kingdom come, Thy will be done in earth,
as it is in heaven.
Give us this day our daily bread.
And forgive us our debts, as we forgive our debtors.
And lead us not into temptation, but deliver us from evil:
For thine is the kingdom, and the power,
and the glory, forever.
Amen.

Psalm for Prayer: Psalm 24

Going Deeper:

- Listen Long and Listen Hard. Lean into what the Lord is saying to you.
- Write it down. If the God of the Universe speaks to you, you might want to write it down.
- Hold it, turn it, and chew it.
- Act on it. Celebrate, Repent, Change.
- Share it.

Notes:

Day 25

Slowly Read: Matthew 25

Questions for Reflection:

Can you notice what Jesus was saying to those he spoke to when it was written?

Which word stood out to you?

Which person or persons stood out to you?

What encouraged you?

What convicted you?

What is the Holy Spirit saying to you through this text?

Pause to pray these into your life:

Pray the Lords' Prayer
Mt 6: 9-13 (KJV)

Our Father which art in heaven, Hallowed be thy name.
Thy kingdom come, Thy will be done in earth,
as it is in heaven.
Give us this day our daily bread.
And forgive us our debts, as we forgive our debtors.
And lead us not into temptation, but deliver us from evil:
For thine is the kingdom, and the power,
and the glory, forever.
Amen.

Psalm for Prayer: Psalm 25

Going Deeper:

- Listen Long and Listen Hard. Lean into what the Lord is saying to you.
- Write it down. If the God of the Universe speaks to you, you might want to write it down.
- Hold it, turn it, and chew it.
- Act on it. Celebrate, Repent, Change.
- Share it.

Notes:

Day 26

Slowly Read: Matthew 26

Questions for Reflection:

Can you notice what Jesus was saying to those he spoke to when it was written?

Which word stood out to you?

Which person or persons stood out to you?

What encouraged you?

What convicted you?

What is the Holy Spirit saying to you through this text?

Pause to pray these into your life:

Pray the Lords' Prayer
Mt 6: 9-13 (KJV)

Our Father which art in heaven, Hallowed be thy name.
Thy kingdom come, Thy will be done in earth,
as it is in heaven.
Give us this day our daily bread.
And forgive us our debts, as we forgive our debtors.
And lead us not into temptation, but deliver us from evil:
For thine is the kingdom, and the power,
and the glory, forever.
Amen.

Psalm for Prayer: Psalm 26

Going Deeper:

- Listen Long and Listen Hard. Lean into what the Lord is saying to you.
- Write it down. If the God of the Universe speaks to you, you might want to write it down.
- Hold it, turn it, and chew it.
- Act on it. Celebrate, Repent, Change.
- Share it.

Notes:

Day 27

Slowly Read: Matthew 27

Questions for Reflection:

Can you notice what Jesus was saying to those he spoke to when it was written?

Which word stood out to you?

Which person or persons stood out to you?

What encouraged you?

What convicted you?

What is the Holy Spirit saying to you through this text?

Pause to pray these into your life:

Pray the Lords' Prayer
Mt 6: 9-13 (KJV)

Our Father which art in heaven, Hallowed be thy name.
Thy kingdom come, Thy will be done in earth,
as it is in heaven.
Give us this day our daily bread.
And forgive us our debts, as we forgive our debtors.
And lead us not into temptation, but deliver us from evil:
For thine is the kingdom, and the power,
and the glory, forever.
Amen.

Psalm for Prayer: Psalm 27

Going Deeper:

- Listen Long and Listen Hard. Lean into what the Lord is saying to you.
- Write it down. If the God of the Universe speaks to you, you might want to write it down.
- Hold it, turn it, and chew it.
- Act on it. Celebrate, Repent, Change.
- Share it.

Notes:

Day 28

Slowly Read: Matthew 28

Questions for Reflection:

Can you notice what Jesus was saying to those he spoke to when it was written?

Which word stood out to you?

Which person or persons stood out to you?

What encouraged you?

What convicted you?

What is the Holy Spirit saying to you through this text?

Pause to pray these into your life:

Pray the Lords' Prayer
Mt 6: 9-13 (KJV)

Our Father which art in heaven, Hallowed be thy name.
Thy kingdom come, Thy will be done in earth,
as it is in heaven.
Give us this day our daily bread.
And forgive us our debts, as we forgive our debtors.
And lead us not into temptation, but deliver us from evil:
For thine is the kingdom, and the power,
and the glory, forever.
Amen.

Psalm for Prayer: Psalm 28

Going Deeper:

- Listen Long and Listen Hard. Lean into what the Lord is saying to you.
- Write it down. If the God of the Universe speaks to you, you might want to write it down.
- Hold it, turn it, and chew it.
- Act on it. Celebrate, Repent, Change.
- Share it.

Notes:

Day 29

Slowly Read: Mark 1

Questions for Reflection:

Can you notice what Jesus was saying to those he spoke to when it was written?

Which word stood out to you?

Which person or persons stood out to you?

What encouraged you?

What convicted you?

What is the Holy Spirit saying to you through this text?

Pause to pray these into your life:

Pray the Lords' Prayer
Mt 6: 9-13 (KJV)

Our Father which art in heaven, Hallowed be thy name.
Thy kingdom come, Thy will be done in earth,
as it is in heaven.
Give us this day our daily bread.
And forgive us our debts, as we forgive our debtors.
And lead us not into temptation, but deliver us from evil:
For thine is the kingdom, and the power,
and the glory, forever.
Amen.

Psalm for Prayer: Psalm 29

Going Deeper:

- Listen Long and Listen Hard. Lean into what the Lord is saying to you.
- Write it down. If the God of the Universe speaks to you, you might want to write it down.
- Hold it, turn it, and chew it.
- Act on it. Celebrate, Repent, Change.
- Share it.

Notes:

Day 30

Slowly Read: Mark 2

Questions for Reflection:

Can you notice what Jesus was saying to those he spoke to when it was written?

Which word stood out to you?

Which person or persons stood out to you?

What encouraged you?

What convicted you?

What is the Holy Spirit saying to you through this text?

Pause to pray these into your life:

Pray the Lords' Prayer
Mt 6: 9-13 (KJV)

Our Father which art in heaven, Hallowed be thy name.
Thy kingdom come, Thy will be done in earth,
as it is in heaven.
Give us this day our daily bread.
And forgive us our debts, as we forgive our debtors.
And lead us not into temptation, but deliver us from evil:
For thine is the kingdom, and the power,
and the glory, forever.
Amen.

Psalm for Prayer: Psalm 30

Going Deeper:

- Listen Long and Listen Hard. Lean into what the Lord is saying to you.
- Write it down. If the God of the Universe speaks to you, you might want to write it down.
- Hold it, turn it, and chew it.
- Act on it. Celebrate, Repent, Change.
- Share it.

Notes:

Day 31

Slowly Read: Mark 3

Questions for Reflection:

Can you notice what Jesus was saying to those he spoke to when it was written?

Which word stood out to you?

Which person or persons stood out to you?

What encouraged you?

What convicted you?

What is the Holy Spirit saying to you through this text?

Pause to pray these into your life:

Pray the Lords' Prayer
Mt 6: 9-13 (KJV)

Our Father which art in heaven, Hallowed be thy name.
Thy kingdom come, Thy will be done in earth,
as it is in heaven.
Give us this day our daily bread.
And forgive us our debts, as we forgive our debtors.
And lead us not into temptation, but deliver us from evil:
For thine is the kingdom, and the power,
and the glory, forever.
Amen.

Psalm for Prayer: Psalm 31

Going Deeper:

- Listen Long and Listen Hard. Lean into what the Lord is saying to you.
- Write it down. If the God of the Universe speaks to you, you might want to write it down.
- Hold it, turn it, and chew it.
- Act on it. Celebrate, Repent, Change.
- Share it.

Notes:

Day 32

Slowly Read: Mark 4

Questions for Reflection:

Can you notice what Jesus was saying to those he spoke to when it was written?

Which word stood out to you?

Which person or persons stood out to you?

What encouraged you?

What convicted you?

What is the Holy Spirit saying to you through this text?

Pause to pray these into your life:

Pray the Lords' Prayer
Mt 6: 9-13 (KJV)

Our Father which art in heaven, Hallowed be thy name.
Thy kingdom come, Thy will be done in earth,
as it is in heaven.
Give us this day our daily bread.
And forgive us our debts, as we forgive our debtors.
And lead us not into temptation, but deliver us from evil:
For thine is the kingdom, and the power,
and the glory, forever.
Amen.

Psalm for Prayer: Psalm 32

Going Deeper:

- Listen Long and Listen Hard. Lean into what the Lord is saying to you.
- Write it down. If the God of the Universe speaks to you, you might want to write it down.
- Hold it, turn it, and chew it.
- Act on it. Celebrate, Repent, Change.
- Share it.

Notes:

Day 33

Slowly Read: Mark 5

Questions for Reflection:

Can you notice what Jesus was saying to those he spoke to when it was written?

Which word stood out to you?

Which person or persons stood out to you?

What encouraged you?

What convicted you?

What is the Holy Spirit saying to you through this text?

Pause to pray these into your life:

Pray the Lords' Prayer
Mt 6: 9-13 (KJV)

Our Father which art in heaven, Hallowed be thy name.
Thy kingdom come, Thy will be done in earth,
as it is in heaven.
Give us this day our daily bread.
And forgive us our debts, as we forgive our debtors.
And lead us not into temptation, but deliver us from evil:
For thine is the kingdom, and the power,
and the glory, forever.
Amen.

Psalm for Prayer: Psalm 33

Going Deeper:

- Listen Long and Listen Hard. Lean into what the Lord is saying to you.
- Write it down. If the God of the Universe speaks to you, you might want to write it down.
- Hold it, turn it, and chew it.
- Act on it. Celebrate, Repent, Change.
- Share it.

Notes

Day 34

Slowly Read: Mark 6

Questions for Reflection:

Can you notice what Jesus was saying to those he spoke to when it was written?

Which word stood out to you?

Which person or persons stood out to you?

What encouraged you?

What convicted you?

What is the Holy Spirit saying to you through this text?

Pause to pray these into your life:

Pray the Lords' Prayer
Mt 6: 9-13 (KJV)

Our Father which art in heaven, Hallowed be thy name.
Thy kingdom come, Thy will be done in earth,
as it is in heaven.
Give us this day our daily bread.
And forgive us our debts, as we forgive our debtors.
And lead us not into temptation, but deliver us from evil:
For thine is the kingdom, and the power,
and the glory, forever.
Amen.

Psalm for Prayer: Psalm 34

Going Deeper:

- Listen Long and Listen Hard. Lean into what the Lord is saying to you.
- Write it down. If the God of the Universe speaks to you, you might want to write it down.
- Hold it, turn it, and chew it.
- Act on it. Celebrate, Repent, Change.
- Share it.

Notes:

Day 35

Slowly Read: Mark 7

Questions for Reflection:

Can you notice what Jesus was saying to those he spoke to when it was written?

Which word stood out to you?

Which person or persons stood out to you?

What encouraged you?

What convicted you?

What is the Holy Spirit saying to you through this text?

Pause to pray these into your life:

Pray the Lords' Prayer
Mt 6: 9-13 (KJV)

Our Father which art in heaven, Hallowed be thy name.
Thy kingdom come, Thy will be done in earth,
as it is in heaven.
Give us this day our daily bread.
And forgive us our debts, as we forgive our debtors.
And lead us not into temptation, but deliver us from evil:
For thine is the kingdom, and the power,
and the glory, forever.
Amen.

Psalm for Prayer: Psalm 35

Going Deeper:

- Listen Long and Listen Hard. Lean into what the Lord is saying to you.
- Write it down. If the God of the Universe speaks to you, you might want to write it down.
- Hold it, turn it, and chew it.
- Act on it. Celebrate, Repent, Change.
- Share it.

Notes:

Day 36

Slowly Read: Mark 8

Questions for Reflection:

Can you notice what Jesus was saying to those he spoke to when it was written?

Which word stood out to you?

Which person or persons stood out to you?

What encouraged you?

What convicted you?

What is the Holy Spirit saying to you through this text?

Pause to pray these into your life:

Pray the Lords' Prayer
Mt 6: 9-13 (KJV)

Our Father which art in heaven, Hallowed be thy name.
Thy kingdom come, Thy will be done in earth,
as it is in heaven.
Give us this day our daily bread.
And forgive us our debts, as we forgive our debtors.
And lead us not into temptation, but deliver us from evil:
For thine is the kingdom, and the power,
and the glory, forever.
Amen.

Psalm for Prayer: Psalm 36

Going Deeper:

- Listen Long and Listen Hard. Lean into what the Lord is saying to you.
- Write it down. If the God of the Universe speaks to you, you might want to write it down.
- Hold it, turn it, and chew it.
- Act on it. Celebrate, Repent, Change.
- Share it.

Notes:

Day 37

Slowly Read: Mark 9

Questions for Reflection:

Can you notice what Jesus was saying to those he spoke to when it was written?

Which word stood out to you?

Which person or persons stood out to you?

What encouraged you?

What convicted you?

What is the Holy Spirit saying to you through this text?

Pause to pray these into your life:

Pray the Lords' Prayer
Mt 6: 9-13 (KJV)

Our Father which art in heaven, Hallowed be thy name.
Thy kingdom come, Thy will be done in earth,
as it is in heaven.
Give us this day our daily bread.
And forgive us our debts, as we forgive our debtors.
And lead us not into temptation, but deliver us from evil:
For thine is the kingdom, and the power,
and the glory, forever.
Amen.

Psalm for Prayer: Psalm 37

Going Deeper:

- Listen Long and Listen Hard. Lean into what the Lord is saying to you.
- Write it down. If the God of the Universe speaks to you, you might want to write it down.
- Hold it, turn it, and chew it.
- Act on it. Celebrate, Repent, Change.
- Share it.

Notes:

Day 38

Slowly Read: Mark 10

Questions for Reflection:

Can you notice what Jesus was saying to those he spoke to when it was written?

Which word stood out to you?

Which person or persons stood out to you?

What encouraged you?

What convicted you?

What is the Holy Spirit saying to you through this text?

Pause to pray these into your life:

Pray the Lords' Prayer
Mt 6: 9-13 (KJV)

Our Father which art in heaven, Hallowed be thy name.
Thy kingdom come, Thy will be done in earth,
as it is in heaven.
Give us this day our daily bread.
And forgive us our debts, as we forgive our debtors.
And lead us not into temptation, but deliver us from evil:
For thine is the kingdom, and the power,
and the glory, forever.
Amen.

Psalm for Prayer: Psalm 38

Going Deeper:

- Listen Long and Listen Hard. Lean into what the Lord is saying to you.
- Write it down. If the God of the Universe speaks to you, you might want to write it down.
- Hold it, turn it, and chew it.
- Act on it. Celebrate, Repent, Change.
- Share it.

Notes:

Day 39

Slowly Read: Mark 11

Questions for Reflection:

Can you notice what Jesus was saying to those he spoke to when it was written?

Which word stood out to you?

Which person or persons stood out to you?

What encouraged you?

What convicted you?

What is the Holy Spirit saying to you through this text?

Pause to pray these into your life:

Pray the Lords' Prayer
Mt 6: 9-13 (KJV)

*Our Father which art in heaven, Hallowed be thy name.
Thy kingdom come, Thy will be done in earth,
as it is in heaven.
Give us this day our daily bread.
And forgive us our debts, as we forgive our debtors.
And lead us not into temptation, but deliver us from evil:
For thine is the kingdom, and the power,
and the glory, forever.
Amen.*

Psalm for Prayer: Psalm 39

Going Deeper:

- Listen Long and Listen Hard. Lean into what the Lord is saying to you.
- Write it down. If the God of the Universe speaks to you, you might want to write it down.
- Hold it, turn it, and chew it.
- Act on it. Celebrate, Repent, Change.
- Share it.

Notes:

Day 40

Slowly Read: Mark 12

Questions for Reflection:

Can you notice what Jesus was saying to those he spoke to when it was written?

Which word stood out to you?

Which person or persons stood out to you?

What encouraged you?

What convicted you?

What is the Holy Spirit saying to you through this text?

Pause to pray these into your life:

Pray the Lords' Prayer
Mt 6: 9-13 (KJV)

Our Father which art in heaven, Hallowed be thy name.
Thy kingdom come, Thy will be done in earth,
as it is in heaven.
Give us this day our daily bread.
And forgive us our debts, as we forgive our debtors.
And lead us not into temptation, but deliver us from evil:
For thine is the kingdom, and the power,
and the glory, forever.
Amen.

Psalm for Prayer: Psalm 40

Going Deeper:

- Listen Long and Listen Hard. Lean into what the Lord is saying to you.
- Write it down. If the God of the Universe speaks to you, you might want to write it down.
- Hold it, turn it, and chew it.
- Act on it. Celebrate, Repent, Change.
- Share it.

Notes:

Day 41

Slowly Read: Mark 13

Questions for Reflection:

Can you notice what Jesus was saying to those he spoke to when it was written?

Which word stood out to you?

Which person or persons stood out to you?

What encouraged you?

What convicted you?

What is the Holy Spirit saying to you through this text?

Pause to pray these into your life:

Pray the Lords' Prayer
Mt 6: 9-13 (KJV)

Our Father which art in heaven, Hallowed be thy name.
Thy kingdom come, Thy will be done in earth,
as it is in heaven.
Give us this day our daily bread.
And forgive us our debts, as we forgive our debtors.
And lead us not into temptation, but deliver us from evil:
For thine is the kingdom, and the power,
and the glory, forever.
Amen.

Psalm for Prayer: Psalm 41

Going Deeper:

- Listen Long and Listen Hard. Lean into what the Lord is saying to you.
- Write it down. If the God of the Universe speaks to you, you might want to write it down.
- Hold it, turn it, and chew it.
- Act on it. Celebrate, Repent, Change.
- Share it.

Notes:

Day 42

Slowly Read: Mark 14

Questions for Reflection:

Can you notice what Jesus was saying to those he spoke to when it was written?

Which word stood out to you?

Which person or persons stood out to you?

What encouraged you?

What convicted you?

What is the Holy Spirit saying to you through this text?

Pause to pray these into your life:

Pray the Lords' Prayer
Mt 6: 9-13 (KJV)

Our Father which art in heaven, Hallowed be thy name.
Thy kingdom come, Thy will be done in earth,
as it is in heaven.
Give us this day our daily bread.
And forgive us our debts, as we forgive our debtors.
And lead us not into temptation, but deliver us from evil:
For thine is the kingdom, and the power,
and the glory, forever.
Amen.

Psalm for Prayer: Psalm 42

Going Deeper:

- Listen Long and Listen Hard. Lean into what the Lord is saying to you.
- Write it down. If the God of the Universe speaks to you, you might want to write it down.
- Hold it, turn it, and chew it.
- Act on it. Celebrate, Repent, Change.
- Share it.

Notes:

Day 43

Slowly Read: Mark 15

Questions for Reflection:

Can you notice what Jesus was saying to those he spoke to when it was written?

Which word stood out to you?

Which person or persons stood out to you?

What encouraged you?

What convicted you?

What is the Holy Spirit saying to you through this text?

Pause to pray these into your life:

Pray the Lords' Prayer
Mt 6: 9-13 (KJV)

Our Father which art in heaven, Hallowed be thy name.
Thy kingdom come, Thy will be done in earth,
as it is in heaven.
Give us this day our daily bread.
And forgive us our debts, as we forgive our debtors.
And lead us not into temptation, but deliver us from evil:
For thine is the kingdom, and the power,
and the glory, forever.
Amen.

Psalm for Prayer: Psalm 43

Going Deeper:

- Listen Long and Listen Hard. Lean into what the Lord is saying to you.
- Write it down. If the God of the Universe speaks to you, you might want to write it down.
- Hold it, turn it, and chew it.
- Act on it. Celebrate, Repent, Change.
- Share it.

Notes:

Day 44

Slowly Read: Mark 16

Questions for Reflection:

Can you notice what Jesus was saying to those he spoke to when it was written?

Which word stood out to you?

Which person or persons stood out to you?

What encouraged you?

What convicted you?

What is the Holy Spirit saying to you through this text?

Pause to pray these into your life:

Pray the Lords' Prayer
Mt 6: 9-13 (KJV)

Our Father which art in heaven, Hallowed be thy name.
Thy kingdom come, Thy will be done in earth,
as it is in heaven.
Give us this day our daily bread.
And forgive us our debts, as we forgive our debtors.
And lead us not into temptation, but deliver us from evil:
For thine is the kingdom, and the power,
and the glory, forever.
Amen.

Psalm for Prayer: Psalm 44

Going Deeper:

- Listen Long and Listen Hard. Lean into what the Lord is saying to you.
- Write it down. If the God of the Universe speaks to you, you might want to write it down.
- Hold it, turn it, and chew it.
- Act on it. Celebrate, Repent, Change.
- Share it.

Notes:

Day 45

Slowly Read: Luke 1:1-40

Questions for Reflection:

Can you notice what Jesus was saying to those he spoke to when it was written?

Which word stood out to you?

Which person or persons stood out to you?

What encouraged you?

What convicted you?

What is the Holy Spirit saying to you through this text?

Pause to pray these into your life:

Pray the Lords' Prayer
Mt 6: 9-13 (KJV)

Our Father which art in heaven, Hallowed be thy name.
Thy kingdom come, Thy will be done in earth,
as it is in heaven.
Give us this day our daily bread.
And forgive us our debts, as we forgive our debtors.
And lead us not into temptation, but deliver us from evil:
For thine is the kingdom, and the power,
and the glory, forever.
Amen.

Psalm for Prayer: Psalm 45

Going Deeper:

• Listen Long and Listen Hard. Lean into what the Lord is saying to you.
• Write it down. If the God of the Universe speaks to you, you might want to write it down.
• Hold it, turn it, and chew it.
• Act on it. Celebrate, Repent, Change.
• Share it.

Notes:

Day 46

Slowly Read: Luke 1:41-80

Questions for Reflection:

Can you notice what Jesus was saying to those he spoke to when it was written?

Which word stood out to you?

Which person or persons stood out to you?

What encouraged you?

What convicted you?

What is the Holy Spirit saying to you through this text?

Pause to pray these into your life:

Pray the Lords' Prayer
Mt 6: 9-13 (KJV)

Our Father which art in heaven, Hallowed be thy name.
Thy kingdom come, Thy will be done in earth,
as it is in heaven.
Give us this day our daily bread.
And forgive us our debts, as we forgive our debtors.
And lead us not into temptation, but deliver us from evil:
For thine is the kingdom, and the power,
and the glory, forever.
Amen.

Psalm for Prayer: Psalm 46

Going Deeper:

- Listen Long and Listen Hard. Lean into what the Lord is saying to you.
- Write it down. If the God of the Universe speaks to you, you might want to write it down.
- Hold it, turn it, and chew it.
- Act on it. Celebrate, Repent, Change.
- Share it.

Notes:

Day 47

Slowly Read: Luke 2

Questions for Reflection:

Can you notice what Jesus was saying to those he spoke to when it was written?

Which word stood out to you?

Which person or persons stood out to you?

What encouraged you?

What convicted you?

What is the Holy Spirit saying to you through this text?

Pause to pray these into your life:

Pray the Lords' Prayer
Mt 6: 9-13 (KJV)

Our Father which art in heaven, Hallowed be thy name.
Thy kingdom come, Thy will be done in earth,
as it is in heaven.
Give us this day our daily bread.
And forgive us our debts, as we forgive our debtors.
And lead us not into temptation, but deliver us from evil:
For thine is the kingdom, and the power,
and the glory, forever.
Amen.

Psalm for Prayer: Psalm 47

Going Deeper:

- Listen Long and Listen Hard. Lean into what the Lord is saying to you.
- Write it down. If the God of the Universe speaks to you, you might want to write it down.
- Hold it, turn it, and chew it.
- Act on it. Celebrate, Repent, Change.
- Share it.

Notes:

Day 48

Slowly Read: Luke 3

Questions for Reflection:

Can you notice what Jesus was saying to those he spoke to when it was written?

Which word stood out to you?

Which person or persons stood out to you?

What encouraged you?

What convicted you?

What is the Holy Spirit saying to you through this text?

Pause to pray these into your life:

Pray the Lords' Prayer
Mt 6: 9-13 (KJV)

Our Father which art in heaven, Hallowed be thy name.
Thy kingdom come, Thy will be done in earth,
as it is in heaven.
Give us this day our daily bread.
And forgive us our debts, as we forgive our debtors.
And lead us not into temptation, but deliver us from evil:
For thine is the kingdom, and the power,
and the glory, forever.
Amen.

Psalm for Prayer: Psalm 48

Going Deeper:

- Listen Long and Listen Hard. Lean into what the Lord is saying to you.
- Write it down. If the God of the Universe speaks to you, you might want to write it down.
- Hold it, turn it, and chew it.
- Act on it. Celebrate, Repent, Change.
- Share it.

Notes:

Day 49

Slowly Read: Luke 4

Questions for Reflection:

Can you notice what Jesus was saying to those he spoke to when it was written?

Which word stood out to you?

Which person or persons stood out to you?

What encouraged you?

What convicted you?

What is the Holy Spirit saying to you through this text?

Pause to pray these into your life:

Pray the Lords' Prayer
Mt 6: 9-13 (KJV)

Our Father which art in heaven, Hallowed be thy name.
Thy kingdom come, Thy will be done in earth,
as it is in heaven.
Give us this day our daily bread.
And forgive us our debts, as we forgive our debtors.
And lead us not into temptation, but deliver us from evil:
For thine is the kingdom, and the power,
and the glory, forever.
Amen.

Psalm for Prayer: Psalm 49

Going Deeper:

- Listen Long and Listen Hard. Lean into what the Lord is saying to you.
- Write it down. If the God of the Universe speaks to you, you might want to write it down.
- Hold it, turn it, and chew it.
- Act on it. Celebrate, Repent, Change.
- Share it.

Notes:

Day 50

Slowly Read: Luke 5

Questions for Reflection:

Can you notice what Jesus was saying to those he spoke to when it was written?

Which word stood out to you?

Which person or persons stood out to you?

What encouraged you?

What convicted you?

What is the Holy Spirit saying to you through this text?

Pause to pray these into your life:

Pray the Lords' Prayer
Mt 6: 9-13 (KJV)

Our Father which art in heaven, Hallowed be thy name.
Thy kingdom come, Thy will be done in earth,
as it is in heaven.
Give us this day our daily bread.
And forgive us our debts, as we forgive our debtors.
And lead us not into temptation, but deliver us from evil:
For thine is the kingdom, and the power,
and the glory, forever.
Amen.

Psalm for Prayer: Psalm 50

Going Deeper:

- Listen Long and Listen Hard. Lean into what the Lord is saying to you.
- Write it down. If the God of the Universe speaks to you, you might want to write it down.
- Hold it, turn it, and chew it.
- Act on it. Celebrate, Repent, Change.
- Share it.

Notes:

Day 51

Slowly Read: Luke 6

Questions for Reflection:

Can you notice what Jesus was saying to those he spoke to when it was written?

Which word stood out to you?

Which person or persons stood out to you?

What encouraged you?

What convicted you?

What is the Holy Spirit saying to you through this text?

Pause to pray these into your life:

Pray the Lords' Prayer
Mt 6: 9-13 (KJV)

Our Father which art in heaven, Hallowed be thy name.
Thy kingdom come, Thy will be done in earth,
as it is in heaven.
Give us this day our daily bread.
And forgive us our debts, as we forgive our debtors.
And lead us not into temptation, but deliver us from evil:
For thine is the kingdom, and the power,
and the glory, forever.
Amen.

Psalm for Prayer: Psalm 51

Going Deeper:

- Listen Long and Listen Hard. Lean into what the Lord is saying to you.
- Write it down. If the God of the Universe speaks to you, you might want to write it down.
- Hold it, turn it, and chew it.
- Act on it. Celebrate, Repent, Change.
- Share it.

Notes:

Day 52

Slowly Read: Luke 7

Questions for Reflection:

Can you notice what Jesus was saying to those he spoke to when it was written?

Which word stood out to you?

Which person or persons stood out to you?

What encouraged you?

What convicted you?

What is the Holy Spirit saying to you through this text?

Pause to pray these into your life:

Pray the Lords' Prayer
Mt 6: 9-13 (KJV)

Our Father which art in heaven, Hallowed be thy name.
Thy kingdom come, Thy will be done in earth,
as it is in heaven.
Give us this day our daily bread.
And forgive us our debts, as we forgive our debtors.
And lead us not into temptation, but deliver us from evil:
For thine is the kingdom, and the power,
and the glory, forever.
Amen.

Psalm for Prayer: Psalm 52

Going Deeper:

- Listen Long and Listen Hard. Lean into what the Lord is saying to you.
- Write it down. If the God of the Universe speaks to you, you might want to write it down.
- Hold it, turn it, and chew it.
- Act on it. Celebrate, Repent, Change.
- Share it.

Notes:

Day 53

Slowly Read: Luke 8

Questions for Reflection:

Can you notice what Jesus was saying to those he spoke to when it was written?

Which word stood out to you?

Which person or persons stood out to you?

What encouraged you?

What convicted you?

What is the Holy Spirit saying to you through this text?

Pause to pray these into your life:

Pray the Lords' Prayer
Mt 6: 9-13 (KJV)

Our Father which art in heaven, Hallowed be thy name.
Thy kingdom come, Thy will be done in earth,
as it is in heaven.
Give us this day our daily bread.
And forgive us our debts, as we forgive our debtors.
And lead us not into temptation, but deliver us from evil:
For thine is the kingdom, and the power,
and the glory, forever.
Amen.

Psalm for Prayer: Psalm 53

Going Deeper:

- Listen Long and Listen Hard. Lean into what the Lord is saying to you.
- Write it down. If the God of the Universe speaks to you, you might want to write it down.
- Hold it, turn it, and chew it.
- Act on it. Celebrate, Repent, Change.
- Share it.

Notes:

Day 54

Slowly Read: Luke 9

Questions for Reflection:

Can you notice what Jesus was saying to those he spoke to when it was written?

Which word stood out to you?

Which person or persons stood out to you?

What encouraged you?

What convicted you?

What is the Holy Spirit saying to you through this text?

Pause to pray these into your life:

Pray the Lords' Prayer
Mt 6: 9-13 (KJV)

Our Father which art in heaven, Hallowed be thy name.
Thy kingdom come, Thy will be done in earth,
as it is in heaven.
Give us this day our daily bread.
And forgive us our debts, as we forgive our debtors.
And lead us not into temptation, but deliver us from evil:
For thine is the kingdom, and the power,
and the glory, forever.
Amen.

Psalm for Prayer: Psalm 54

Going Deeper:

- Listen Long and Listen Hard. Lean into what the Lord is saying to you.
- Write it down. If the God of the Universe speaks to you, you might want to write it down.
- Hold it, turn it, and chew it.
- Act on it. Celebrate, Repent, Change.
- Share it.

Notes:

Day 55

Slowly Read: Luke 10

Questions for Reflection:

Can you notice what Jesus was saying to those he spoke to when it was written?

Which word stood out to you?

Which person or persons stood out to you?

What encouraged you?

What convicted you?

What is the Holy Spirit saying to you through this text?

Pause to pray these into your life:

Psalm for Prayer: Psalm 55

Going Deeper:

* Listen Long and Listen Hard. Lean into what the Lord is saying to you.
* Write it down. If the God of the Universe speaks to you, you might want to write it down.
* Hold it, turn it, and chew it.
* Act on it. Celebrate, Repent, Change.
* Share it.

Notes:

Day 56

Slowly Read: Luke 11

Questions for Reflection:

Can you notice what Jesus was saying to those he spoke to when it was written?

Which word stood out to you?

Which person or persons stood out to you?

What encouraged you?

What convicted you?

What is the Holy Spirit saying to you through this text?

Pause to pray these into your life:

Pray the Lords' Prayer
Mt 6: 9-13 (KJV)

Our Father which art in heaven, Hallowed be thy name.
Thy kingdom come, Thy will be done in earth,
as it is in heaven.
Give us this day our daily bread.
And forgive us our debts, as we forgive our debtors.
And lead us not into temptation, but deliver us from evil:
For thine is the kingdom, and the power,
and the glory, forever.
Amen.

Psalm for Prayer: Psalm 56

Going Deeper:

- Listen Long and Listen Hard. Lean into what the Lord is saying to you.
- Write it down. If the God of the Universe speaks to you, you might want to write it down.
- Hold it, turn it, and chew it.
- Act on it. Celebrate, Repent, Change.
- Share it.

Notes:

Day 57

Slowly Read: Luke 12

Questions for Reflection:

Can you notice what Jesus was saying to those he spoke to when it was written?

Which word stood out to you?

Which person or persons stood out to you?

What encouraged you?

What convicted you?

What is the Holy Spirit saying to you through this text?

Pause to pray these into your life:

Pray the Lords' Prayer
Mt 6: 9-13 (KJV)

Our Father which art in heaven, Hallowed be thy name.
Thy kingdom come, Thy will be done in earth,
as it is in heaven.
Give us this day our daily bread.
And forgive us our debts, as we forgive our debtors.
And lead us not into temptation, but deliver us from evil:
For thine is the kingdom, and the power,
and the glory, forever.
Amen.

Psalm for Prayer: Psalm 57

Going Deeper:

- Listen Long and Listen Hard. Lean into what the Lord is saying to you.
- Write it down. If the God of the Universe speaks to you, you might want to write it down.
- Hold it, turn it, and chew it.
- Act on it. Celebrate, Repent, Change.
- Share it.

Notes:

Day 58

Slowly Read: Luke 13

Questions for Reflection:

Can you notice what Jesus was saying to those he spoke to when it was written?

Which word stood out to you?

Which person or persons stood out to you?

What encouraged you?

What convicted you?

What is the Holy Spirit saying to you through this text?

Pause to pray these into your life:

Pray the Lords' Prayer
Mt 6: 9-13 (KJV)

Our Father which art in heaven, Hallowed be thy name.
Thy kingdom come, Thy will be done in earth,
as it is in heaven.
Give us this day our daily bread.
And forgive us our debts, as we forgive our debtors.
And lead us not into temptation, but deliver us from evil:
For thine is the kingdom, and the power,
and the glory, forever.
Amen.

Psalm for Prayer: Psalm 58

Going Deeper:

- Listen Long and Listen Hard. Lean into what the Lord is saying to you.
- Write it down. If the God of the Universe speaks to you, you might want to write it down.
- Hold it, turn it, and chew it.
- Act on it. Celebrate, Repent, Change.
- Share it.

Notes
;

Day 59

Slowly Read: Luke 14

Questions for Reflection:

Can you notice what Jesus was saying to those he spoke to when it was written?

Which word stood out to you?

Which person or persons stood out to you?

What encouraged you?

What convicted you?

What is the Holy Spirit saying to you through this text?

Pause to pray these into your life:

Pray the Lords' Prayer
Mt 6: 9-13 (KJV)

Our Father which art in heaven, Hallowed be thy name.
Thy kingdom come, Thy will be done in earth,
as it is in heaven.
Give us this day our daily bread.
And forgive us our debts, as we forgive our debtors.
And lead us not into temptation, but deliver us from evil:
For thine is the kingdom, and the power,
and the glory, forever.
Amen.

Psalm for Prayer: Psalm 59

Going Deeper:

- Listen Long and Listen Hard. Lean into what the Lord is saying to you.
- Write it down. If the God of the Universe speaks to you, you might want to write it down.
- Hold it, turn it, and chew it.
- Act on it. Celebrate, Repent, Change.
- Share it.

Notes:

147

Day 60

Slowly Read: Luke 15

Questions for Reflection:

Can you notice what Jesus was saying to those he spoke to when it was written?

Which word stood out to you?

Which person or persons stood out to you?

What encouraged you?

What convicted you?

What is the Holy Spirit saying to you through this text?

Pause to pray these into your life:

Pray the Lords' Prayer
Mt 6: 9-13 (KJV)

Our Father which art in heaven, Hallowed be thy name.
Thy kingdom come, Thy will be done in earth,
as it is in heaven.
Give us this day our daily bread.
And forgive us our debts, as we forgive our debtors.
And lead us not into temptation, but deliver us from evil:
For thine is the kingdom, and the power,
and the glory, forever.
Amen.

Psalm for Prayer: Psalm 60

Going Deeper:

- Listen Long and Listen Hard. Lean into what the Lord is saying to you.
- Write it down. If the God of the Universe speaks to you, you might want to write it down.
- Hold it, turn it, and chew it.
- Act on it. Celebrate, Repent, Change.
- Share it.

Notes:

Day 61

Slowly Read: Luke 16

Questions for Reflection:

Can you notice what Jesus was saying to those he spoke to when it was written?

Which word stood out to you?

Which person or persons stood out to you?

What encouraged you?

What convicted you?

What is the Holy Spirit saying to you through this text?

Pause to pray these into your life:

Pray the Lords' Prayer
Mt 6: 9-13 (KJV)

Our Father which art in heaven, Hallowed be thy name.
Thy kingdom come, Thy will be done in earth,
as it is in heaven.
Give us this day our daily bread.
And forgive us our debts, as we forgive our debtors.
And lead us not into temptation, but deliver us from evil:
For thine is the kingdom, and the power,
and the glory, forever.
Amen.

Psalm for Prayer: Psalm 61

Going Deeper:

- Listen Long and Listen Hard. Lean into what the Lord is saying to you.
- Write it down. If the God of the Universe speaks to you, you might want to write it down.
- Hold it, turn it, and chew it.
- Act on it. Celebrate, Repent, Change.
- Share it.

Notes:

Day 62

Slowly Read: Luke 17

Questions for Reflection:

Can you notice what Jesus was saying to those he spoke to when it was written?

Which word stood out to you?

Which person or persons stood out to you?

What encouraged you?

What convicted you?

What is the Holy Spirit saying to you through this text?

Pause to pray these into your life:

Pray the Lords' Prayer
Mt 6: 9-13 (KJV)

Our Father which art in heaven, Hallowed be thy name.
Thy kingdom come, Thy will be done in earth,
as it is in heaven.
Give us this day our daily bread.
And forgive us our debts, as we forgive our debtors.
And lead us not into temptation, but deliver us from evil:
For thine is the kingdom, and the power,
and the glory, forever.
Amen.

Psalm for Prayer: Psalm 62

Going Deeper:

- Listen Long and Listen Hard. Lean into what the Lord is saying to you.
- Write it down. If the God of the Universe speaks to you, you might want to write it down.
- Hold it, turn it, and chew it.
- Act on it. Celebrate, Repent, Change.
- Share it.

Notes:

Day 63

Slowly Read: Luke 18

Questions for Reflection:

Can you notice what Jesus was saying to those he spoke to when it was written?

Which word stood out to you?

Which person or persons stood out to you?

What encouraged you?

What convicted you?

What is the Holy Spirit saying to you through this text?

Pause to pray these into your life:

Pray the Lords' Prayer
Mt 6: 9-13 (KJV)

Our Father which art in heaven, Hallowed be thy name.
Thy kingdom come, Thy will be done in earth,
as it is in heaven.
Give us this day our daily bread.
And forgive us our debts, as we forgive our debtors.
And lead us not into temptation, but deliver us from evil:
For thine is the kingdom, and the power,
and the glory, forever.
Amen.

Psalm for Prayer: Psalm 63

Going Deeper:

- Listen Long and Listen Hard. Lean into what the Lord is saying to you.
- Write it down. If the God of the Universe speaks to you, you might want to write it down.
- Hold it, turn it, and chew it.
- Act on it. Celebrate, Repent, Change.
- Share it.

Notes:

Day 64

Slowly Read: Luke 19

Questions for Reflection:

Can you notice what Jesus was saying to those he spoke to when it was written?

Which word stood out to you?

Which person or persons stood out to you?

What encouraged you?

What convicted you?

What is the Holy Spirit saying to you through this text?

Pause to pray these into your life:

Psalm for Prayer: Psalm 64

Going Deeper:

- Listen Long and Listen Hard. Lean into what the Lord is saying to you.
- Write it down. If the God of the Universe speaks to you, you might want to write it down.
- Hold it, turn it, and chew it.
- Act on it. Celebrate, Repent, Change.
- Share it.

Notes:

Day 65

Slowly Read: Luke 20

Questions for Reflection:

Can you notice what Jesus was saying to those he spoke to when it was written?

Which word stood out to you?

Which person or persons stood out to you?

What encouraged you?

What convicted you?

What is the Holy Spirit saying to you through this text?

Pause to pray these into your life:

Pray the Lords' Prayer
Mt 6: 9-13 (KJV)

Our Father which art in heaven, Hallowed be thy name.
Thy kingdom come, Thy will be done in earth,
as it is in heaven.
Give us this day our daily bread.
And forgive us our debts, as we forgive our debtors.
And lead us not into temptation, but deliver us from evil:
For thine is the kingdom, and the power,
and the glory, forever.
Amen.

Psalm for Prayer: Psalm 65

Going Deeper:

- Listen Long and Listen Hard. Lean into what the Lord is saying to you.
- Write it down. If the God of the Universe speaks to you, you might want to write it down.
- Hold it, turn it, and chew it.
- Act on it. Celebrate, Repent, Change.
- Share it.

Notes:

Day 66

Slowly Read: Luke 21

Questions for Reflection:

Can you notice what Jesus was saying to those he spoke to when it was written?

Which word stood out to you?

Which person or persons stood out to you?

What encouraged you?

What convicted you?

What is the Holy Spirit saying to you through this text?

Pause to pray these into your life:

Pray the Lords' Prayer
Mt 6: 9-13 (KJV)

Our Father which art in heaven, Hallowed be thy name.
Thy kingdom come, Thy will be done in earth,
as it is in heaven.
Give us this day our daily bread.
And forgive us our debts, as we forgive our debtors.
And lead us not into temptation, but deliver us from evil:
For thine is the kingdom, and the power,
and the glory, forever.
Amen.

Psalm for Prayer: Psalm 66

Going Deeper:

- Listen Long and Listen Hard. Lean into what the Lord is saying to you.
- Write it down. If the God of the Universe speaks to you, you might want to write it down.
- Hold it, turn it, and chew it.
- Act on it. Celebrate, Repent, Change.
- Share it.

Notes:

Day 67

Slowly Read: Luke 22

Questions for Reflection:

Can you notice what Jesus was saying to those he spoke to when it was written?

Which word stood out to you?

Which person or persons stood out to you?

What encouraged you?

What convicted you?

What is the Holy Spirit saying to you through this text?

Pause to pray these into your life:

Pray the Lords' Prayer
Mt 6: 9-13 (KJV)

Our Father which art in heaven, Hallowed be thy name.
Thy kingdom come, Thy will be done in earth,
as it is in heaven.
Give us this day our daily bread.
And forgive us our debts, as we forgive our debtors.
And lead us not into temptation, but deliver us from evil:
For thine is the kingdom, and the power,
and the glory, forever.
Amen.

Psalm for Prayer: Psalm 67

Going Deeper:

- Listen Long and Listen Hard. Lean into what the Lord is saying to you.
- Write it down. If the God of the Universe speaks to you, you might want to write it down.
- Hold it, turn it, and chew it.
- Act on it. Celebrate, Repent, Change.
- Share it.

Notes:

Day 68

Slowly Read: Luke 23

Questions for Reflection:

Can you notice what Jesus was saying to those he spoke to when it was written?

Which word stood out to you?

Which person or persons stood out to you?

What encouraged you?

What convicted you?

What is the Holy Spirit saying to you through this text?

Pause to pray these into your life:

Pray the Lords' Prayer
Mt 6: 9-13 (KJV)

Our Father which art in heaven, Hallowed be thy name.
Thy kingdom come, Thy will be done in earth,
as it is in heaven.
Give us this day our daily bread.
And forgive us our debts, as we forgive our debtors.
And lead us not into temptation, but deliver us from evil:
For thine is the kingdom, and the power,
and the glory, forever.
Amen.

Psalm for Prayer: Psalm 68

Going Deeper:

- Listen Long and Listen Hard. Lean into what the Lord is saying to you.
- Write it down. If the God of the Universe speaks to you, you might want to write it down.
- Hold it, turn it, and chew it.
- Act on it. Celebrate, Repent, Change.
- Share it.

Notes:

Day 69

Slowly Read: Luke 24

Questions for Reflection:

Can you notice what Jesus was saying to those he spoke to when it was written?

Which word stood out to you?

Which person or persons stood out to you?

What encouraged you?

What convicted you?

What is the Holy Spirit saying to you through this text?

Pause to pray these into your life:

Pray the Lords' Prayer
Mt 6: 9-13 (KJV)

Our Father which art in heaven, Hallowed be thy name.
Thy kingdom come, Thy will be done in earth,
as it is in heaven.
Give us this day our daily bread.
And forgive us our debts, as we forgive our debtors.
And lead us not into temptation, but deliver us from evil:
For thine is the kingdom, and the power,
and the glory, forever.
Amen.

Psalm for Prayer: Psalm 69

Going Deeper:

- Listen Long and Listen Hard. Lean into what the Lord is saying to you.
- Write it down. If the God of the Universe speaks to you, you might want to write it down.
- Hold it, turn it, and chew it.
- Act on it. Celebrate, Repent, Change.
- Share it.

Notes:

Day 70

Slowly Read: John 1

Questions for Reflection:

Can you notice what Jesus was saying to those he spoke to when it was written?

Which word stood out to you?

Which person or persons stood out to you?

What encouraged you?

What convicted you?

What is the Holy Spirit saying to you through this text?

Pause to pray these into your life:

Pray the Lords' Prayer
Mt 6: 9-13 (KJV)

Our Father which art in heaven, Hallowed be thy name.
Thy kingdom come, Thy will be done in earth,
as it is in heaven.
Give us this day our daily bread.
And forgive us our debts, as we forgive our debtors.
And lead us not into temptation, but deliver us from evil:
For thine is the kingdom, and the power,
and the glory, forever.
Amen.

Psalm for Prayer: Psalm 70

Going Deeper:

*   Listen Long and Listen Hard. Lean into what the Lord is saying to you.
*   Write it down. If the God of the Universe speaks to you, you might want to write it down.
*   Hold it, turn it, and chew it.
*   Act on it. Celebrate, Repent, Change.
*   Share it.

Notes:

Day 71

Slowly Read: John 2

Questions for Reflection:

Can you notice what Jesus was saying to those he spoke to when it was written?

Which word stood out to you?

Which person or persons stood out to you?

What encouraged you?

What convicted you?

What is the Holy Spirit saying to you through this text?

Pause to pray these into your life:

Pray the Lords' Prayer
Mt 6: 9-13 (KJV)

Our Father which art in heaven, Hallowed be thy name.
Thy kingdom come, Thy will be done in earth,
as it is in heaven.
Give us this day our daily bread.
And forgive us our debts, as we forgive our debtors.
And lead us not into temptation, but deliver us from evil:
For thine is the kingdom, and the power,
and the glory, forever.
Amen.

Psalm for Prayer: Psalm 71

Going Deeper:

- Listen Long and Listen Hard. Lean into what the Lord is saying to you.
- Write it down. If the God of the Universe speaks to you, you might want to write it down.
- Hold it, turn it, and chew it.
- Act on it. Celebrate, Repent, Change.
- Share it.

Notes:

Day 72

Slowly Read: John 3

Questions for Reflection:

Can you notice what Jesus was saying to those he spoke to when it was written?

Which word stood out to you?

Which person or persons stood out to you?

What encouraged you?

What convicted you?

What is the Holy Spirit saying to you through this text?

Pause to pray these into your life:

Pray the Lords' Prayer
Mt 6: 9-13 (KJV)

Our Father which art in heaven, Hallowed be thy name.
Thy kingdom come, Thy will be done in earth,
as it is in heaven.
Give us this day our daily bread.
And forgive us our debts, as we forgive our debtors.
And lead us not into temptation, but deliver us from evil:
For thine is the kingdom, and the power,
and the glory, forever.
Amen.

Psalm for Prayer: Psalm 72

Going Deeper:

- Listen Long and Listen Hard. Lean into what the Lord is saying to you.
- Write it down. If the God of the Universe speaks to you, you might want to write it down.
- Hold it, turn it, and chew it.
- Act on it. Celebrate, Repent, Change.
- Share it.

Notes:

Day 73

Slowly Read: John 4

Questions for Reflection:

Can you notice what Jesus was saying to those he spoke to when it was written?

Which word stood out to you?

Which person or persons stood out to you?

What encouraged you?

What convicted you?

What is the Holy Spirit saying to you through this text?

Pause to pray these into your life:

Pray the Lords' Prayer
Mt 6: 9-13 (KJV)

Our Father which art in heaven, Hallowed be thy name.
Thy kingdom come, Thy will be done in earth,
as it is in heaven.
Give us this day our daily bread.
And forgive us our debts, as we forgive our debtors.
And lead us not into temptation, but deliver us from evil:
For thine is the kingdom, and the power,
and the glory, forever.
Amen.

Psalm for Prayer: Psalm 73

Going Deeper:

- Listen Long and Listen Hard. Lean into what the Lord is saying to you.
- Write it down. If the God of the Universe speaks to you, you might want to write it down.
- Hold it, turn it, and chew it.
- Act on it. Celebrate, Repent, Change.
- Share it.

Notes:

Day 74

Slowly Read: John 5

Questions for Reflection:

Can you notice what Jesus was saying to those he spoke to when it was written?

Which word stood out to you?

Which person or persons stood out to you?

What encouraged you?

What convicted you?

What is the Holy Spirit saying to you through this text?

Pause to pray these into your life:

Pray the Lords' Prayer
Mt 6: 9-13 (KJV)

Our Father which art in heaven, Hallowed be thy name.
Thy kingdom come, Thy will be done in earth,
as it is in heaven.
Give us this day our daily bread.
And forgive us our debts, as we forgive our debtors.
And lead us not into temptation, but deliver us from evil:
For thine is the kingdom, and the power,
and the glory, forever.
Amen.

Psalm for Prayer: Psalm 74

Going Deeper:

- Listen Long and Listen Hard. Lean into what the Lord is saying to you.
- Write it down. If the God of the Universe speaks to you, you might want to write it down.
- Hold it, turn it, and chew it.
- Act on it. Celebrate, Repent, Change.
- Share it.

Notes:

177

Day 75

Slowly Read: John 6

Questions for Reflection:

Can you notice what Jesus was saying to those he spoke to when it was written?

Which word stood out to you?

Which person or persons stood out to you?

What encouraged you?

What convicted you?

What is the Holy Spirit saying to you through this text?

Pause to pray these into your life:

Psalm for Prayer: Psalm 75

Going Deeper:

- Listen Long and Listen Hard. Lean into what the Lord is saying to you.
- Write it down. If the God of the Universe speaks to you, you might want to write it down.
- Hold it, turn it, and chew it.
- Act on it. Celebrate, Repent, Change.
- Share it.

Notes:

Day 76

Slowly Read: John 7

Questions for Reflection:

Can you notice what Jesus was saying to those he spoke to when it was written?

Which word stood out to you?

Which person or persons stood out to you?

What encouraged you?

What convicted you?

What is the Holy Spirit saying to you through this text?

Pause to pray these into your life:

Pray the Lords' Prayer
Mt 6: 9-13 (KJV)

Our Father which art in heaven, Hallowed be thy name.
Thy kingdom come, Thy will be done in earth,
as it is in heaven.
Give us this day our daily bread.
And forgive us our debts, as we forgive our debtors.
And lead us not into temptation, but deliver us from evil:
For thine is the kingdom, and the power,
and the glory, forever.
Amen.

Psalm for Prayer: Psalm 76

Going Deeper:

- Listen Long and Listen Hard. Lean into what the Lord is saying to you.
- Write it down. If the God of the Universe speaks to you, you might want to write it down.
- Hold it, turn it, and chew it.
- Act on it. Celebrate, Repent, Change.
- Share it.

Notes:

Day 77

Slowly Read: John 8

Questions for Reflection:

Can you notice what Jesus was saying to those he spoke to when it was written?

Which word stood out to you?

Which person or persons stood out to you?

What encouraged you?

What convicted you?

What is the Holy Spirit saying to you through this text?

Pause to pray these into your life:

Pray the Lords' Prayer
Mt 6: 9-13 (KJV)

Our Father which art in heaven, Hallowed be thy name.
Thy kingdom come, Thy will be done in earth,
as it is in heaven.
Give us this day our daily bread.
And forgive us our debts, as we forgive our debtors.
And lead us not into temptation, but deliver us from evil:
For thine is the kingdom, and the power,
and the glory, forever.
Amen.

Psalm for Prayer: Psalm 77

Going Deeper:

- Listen Long and Listen Hard. Lean into what the Lord is saying to you.
- Write it down. If the God of the Universe speaks to you, you might want to write it down.
- Hold it, turn it, and chew it.
- Act on it. Celebrate, Repent, Change.
- Share it.

Notes:

Day 78

Slowly Read: John 9

Questions for Reflection:

Can you notice what Jesus was saying to those he spoke to when it was written?

Which word stood out to you?

Which person or persons stood out to you?

What encouraged you?

What convicted you?

What is the Holy Spirit saying to you through this text?

Pause to pray these into your life:

Pray the Lords' Prayer
Mt 6: 9-13 (KJV)

Our Father which art in heaven, Hallowed be thy name.
Thy kingdom come, Thy will be done in earth,
as it is in heaven.
Give us this day our daily bread.
And forgive us our debts, as we forgive our debtors.
And lead us not into temptation, but deliver us from evil:
For thine is the kingdom, and the power,
and the glory, forever.
Amen.

Psalm for Prayer: Psalm 78

Going Deeper:

- Listen Long and Listen Hard. Lean into what the Lord is saying to you.
- Write it down. If the God of the Universe speaks to you, you might want to write it down.
- Hold it, turn it, and chew it.
- Act on it. Celebrate, Repent, Change.
- Share it.

Note

Day 79

Slowly Read: John 10

Questions for Reflection:

Can you notice what Jesus was saying to those he spoke to when it was written?

Which word stood out to you?

Which person or persons stood out to you?

What encouraged you?

What convicted you?

What is the Holy Spirit saying to you through this text?

Pause to pray these into your life:

Pray the Lords' Prayer
Mt 6: 9-13 (KJV)

Our Father which art in heaven, Hallowed be thy name.
Thy kingdom come, Thy will be done in earth,
as it is in heaven.
Give us this day our daily bread.
And forgive us our debts, as we forgive our debtors.
And lead us not into temptation, but deliver us from evil:
For thine is the kingdom, and the power,
and the glory, forever.
Amen.

Psalm for Prayer: Psalm 79

Going Deeper:

- Listen Long and Listen Hard. Lean into what the Lord is saying to you.
- Write it down. If the God of the Universe speaks to you, you might want to write it down.
- Hold it, turn it, and chew it.
- Act on it. Celebrate, Repent, Change.
- Share it.

Notes:

Day 80

Slowly Read: John 11

Questions for Reflection:

Can you notice what Jesus was saying to those he spoke to when it was written?

Which word stood out to you?

Which person or persons stood out to you?

What encouraged you?

What convicted you?

What is the Holy Spirit saying to you through this text?

Pause to pray these into your life:

Pray the Lords' Prayer
Mt 6: 9-13 (KJV)

Our Father which art in heaven, Hallowed be thy name.
Thy kingdom come, Thy will be done in earth,
as it is in heaven.
Give us this day our daily bread.
And forgive us our debts, as we forgive our debtors.
And lead us not into temptation, but deliver us from evil:
For thine is the kingdom, and the power,
and the glory, forever.
Amen.

Psalm for Prayer: Psalm 80

Going Deeper:

- Listen Long and Listen Hard. Lean into what the Lord is saying to you.
- Write it down. If the God of the Universe speaks to you, you might want to write it down.
- Hold it, turn it, and chew it.
- Act on it. Celebrate, Repent, Change.
- Share it.

Notes:

189

Day 81

Slowly Read: John 12

Questions for Reflection:

Can you notice what Jesus was saying to those he spoke to when it was written?

Which word stood out to you?

Which person or persons stood out to you?

What encouraged you?

What convicted you?

What is the Holy Spirit saying to you through this text?

Pause to pray these into your life:

Pray the Lords' Prayer
Mt 6: 9-13 (KJV)

Our Father which art in heaven, Hallowed be thy name.
Thy kingdom come, Thy will be done in earth,
as it is in heaven.
Give us this day our daily bread.
And forgive us our debts, as we forgive our debtors.
And lead us not into temptation, but deliver us from evil:
For thine is the kingdom, and the power,
and the glory, forever.
Amen.

Psalm for Prayer: Psalm 81

Going Deeper:

- Listen Long and Listen Hard. Lean into what the Lord is saying to you.
- Write it down. If the God of the Universe speaks to you, you might want to write it down.
- Hold it, turn it, and chew it.
- Act on it. Celebrate, Repent, Change.
- Share it.

Notes:

Day 82

Slowly Read: John 13

Questions for Reflection:

Can you notice what Jesus was saying to those he spoke to when it was written?

Which word stood out to you?

Which person or persons stood out to you?

What encouraged you?

What convicted you?

What is the Holy Spirit saying to you through this text?

Pause to pray these into your life:

Pray the Lords' Prayer
Mt 6: 9-13 (KJV)

Our Father which art in heaven, Hallowed be thy name.
Thy kingdom come, Thy will be done in earth,
as it is in heaven.
Give us this day our daily bread.
And forgive us our debts, as we forgive our debtors.
And lead us not into temptation, but deliver us from evil:
For thine is the kingdom, and the power,
and the glory, forever.
Amen.

Psalm for Prayer: Psalm 82

Going Deeper:

* Listen Long and Listen Hard. Lean into what the Lord is saying to you.
* Write it down. If the God of the Universe speaks to you, you might want to write it down.
* Hold it, turn it, and chew it.
* Act on it. Celebrate, Repent, Change.
* Share it.

Notes:

Day 83

Slowly Read: John 14

Questions for Reflection:

Can you notice what Jesus was saying to those he spoke to when it was written?

Which word stood out to you?

Which person or persons stood out to you?

What encouraged you?

What convicted you?

What is the Holy Spirit saying to you through this text?

Pause to pray these into your life:

Pray the Lords' Prayer
Mt 6: 9-13 (KJV)

Our Father which art in heaven, Hallowed be thy name.
Thy kingdom come, Thy will be done in earth,
as it is in heaven.
Give us this day our daily bread.
And forgive us our debts, as we forgive our debtors.
And lead us not into temptation, but deliver us from evil:
For thine is the kingdom, and the power,
and the glory, forever.
Amen.

Psalm for Prayer: Psalm 83

Going Deeper:

- Listen Long and Listen Hard. Lean into what the Lord is saying to you.
- Write it down. If the God of the Universe speaks to you, you might want to write it down.
- Hold it, turn it, and chew it.
- Act on it. Celebrate, Repent, Change.
- Share it.

Notes:

Day 84

Slowly Read: John 15

Questions for Reflection:

Can you notice what Jesus was saying to those he spoke to when it was written?

Which word stood out to you?

Which person or persons stood out to you?

What encouraged you?

What convicted you?

What is the Holy Spirit saying to you through this text?

Pause to pray these into your life:

Pray the Lords' Prayer
Mt 6: 9-13 (KJV)

Our Father which art in heaven, Hallowed be thy name.
Thy kingdom come, Thy will be done in earth,
as it is in heaven.
Give us this day our daily bread.
And forgive us our debts, as we forgive our debtors.
And lead us not into temptation, but deliver us from evil:
For thine is the kingdom, and the power,
and the glory, forever.
Amen.

Psalm for Prayer: Psalm 84

Going Deeper:

- Listen Long and Listen Hard. Lean into what the Lord is saying to you.
- Write it down. If the God of the Universe speaks to you, you might want to write it down.
- Hold it, turn it, and chew it.
- Act on it. Celebrate, Repent, Change.
- Share it.

Notes:

Day 85

Slowly Read: John 16

Questions for Reflection:

Can you notice what Jesus was saying to those he spoke to when it was written?

Which word stood out to you?

Which person or persons stood out to you?

What encouraged you?

What convicted you?

What is the Holy Spirit saying to you through this text?

Pause to pray these into your life:

Pray the Lords' Prayer
Mt 6: 9-13 (KJV)

Our Father which art in heaven, Hallowed be thy name.
Thy kingdom come, Thy will be done in earth,
as it is in heaven.
Give us this day our daily bread.
And forgive us our debts, as we forgive our debtors.
And lead us not into temptation, but deliver us from evil:
For thine is the kingdom, and the power,
and the glory, forever.
Amen.

Psalm for Prayer: Psalm 85

Going Deeper:

- Listen Long and Listen Hard. Lean into what the Lord is saying to you.
- Write it down. If the God of the Universe speaks to you, you might want to write it down.
- Hold it, turn it, and chew it.
- Act on it. Celebrate, Repent, Change.
- Share it.

Notes:

Day 86

Slowly Read: John 17

Questions for Reflection:

Can you notice what Jesus was saying to those he spoke to when it was written?

Which word stood out to you?

Which person or persons stood out to you?

What encouraged you?

What convicted you?

What is the Holy Spirit saying to you through this text?

Pause to pray these into your life:

Pray the Lords' Prayer
Mt 6: 9-13 (KJV)

Our Father which art in heaven, Hallowed be thy name.
Thy kingdom come, Thy will be done in earth,
as it is in heaven.
Give us this day our daily bread.
And forgive us our debts, as we forgive our debtors.
And lead us not into temptation, but deliver us from evil:
For thine is the kingdom, and the power,
and the glory, forever.
Amen.

Psalm for Prayer: Psalm 86

Going Deeper:

- Listen Long and Listen Hard. Lean into what the Lord is saying to you.
- Write it down. If the God of the Universe speaks to you, you might want to write it down.
- Hold it, turn it, and chew it.
- Act on it. Celebrate, Repent, Change.
- Share it.

Notes:

Day 87

Slowly Read: John 18

Questions for Reflection:

Can you notice what Jesus was saying to those he spoke to when it was written?

Which word stood out to you?

Which person or persons stood out to you?

What encouraged you?

What convicted you?

What is the Holy Spirit saying to you through this text?

Pause to pray these into your life:

Pray the Lords' Prayer
Mt 6: 9-13 (KJV)

Our Father which art in heaven, Hallowed be thy name.
Thy kingdom come, Thy will be done in earth,
as it is in heaven.
Give us this day our daily bread.
And forgive us our debts, as we forgive our debtors.
And lead us not into temptation, but deliver us from evil:
For thine is the kingdom, and the power,
and the glory, forever.
Amen.

Psalm for Prayer: Psalm 87

Going Deeper:

- Listen Long and Listen Hard. Lean into what the Lord is saying to you.
- Write it down. If the God of the Universe speaks to you, you might want to write it down.
- Hold it, turn it, and chew it.
- Act on it. Celebrate, Repent, Change.
- Share it.

Notes:

Day 88

Slowly Read: John 19

Questions for Reflection:

Can you notice what Jesus was saying to those he spoke to when it was written?

Which word stood out to you?

Which person or persons stood out to you?

What encouraged you?

What convicted you?

What is the Holy Spirit saying to you through this text?

Pause to pray these into your life:

Pray the Lords' Prayer
Mt 6: 9-13 (KJV)

Our Father which art in heaven, Hallowed be thy name.
Thy kingdom come, Thy will be done in earth,
as it is in heaven.
Give us this day our daily bread.
And forgive us our debts, as we forgive our debtors.
And lead us not into temptation, but deliver us from evil:
For thine is the kingdom, and the power,
and the glory, forever.
Amen.

Psalm for Prayer: Psalm 88

Going Deeper:

- Listen Long and Listen Hard. Lean into what the Lord is saying to you.
- Write it down. If the God of the Universe speaks to you, you might want to write it down.
- Hold it, turn it, and chew it.
- Act on it. Celebrate, Repent, Change.
- Share it.

Notes:

Day 89

Slowly Read: John 20

Questions for Reflection:

Can you notice what Jesus was saying to those he spoke to when it was written?

Which word stood out to you?

Which person or persons stood out to you?

What encouraged you?

What convicted you?

What is the Holy Spirit saying to you through this text?

Pause to pray these into your life:

Pray the Lords' Prayer
Mt 6: 9-13 (KJV)

Our Father which art in heaven, Hallowed be thy name.
Thy kingdom come, Thy will be done in earth,
as it is in heaven.
Give us this day our daily bread.
And forgive us our debts, as we forgive our debtors.
And lead us not into temptation, but deliver us from evil:
For thine is the kingdom, and the power,
and the glory, forever.
Amen.

Psalm for Prayer: Psalm 89

Going Deeper:

- Listen Long and Listen Hard. Lean into what the Lord is saying to you.
- Write it down. If the God of the Universe speaks to you, you might want to write it down.
- Hold it, turn it, and chew it.
- Act on it. Celebrate, Repent, Change.
- Share it.

Notes:

Day 90

Slowly Read: John 21

Questions for Reflection:

Can you notice what Jesus was saying to those he spoke to when it was written?

Which word stood out to you?

Which person or persons stood out to you?

What encouraged you?

What convicted you?

What is the Holy Spirit saying to you through this text?

Pause to pray these into your life:

Pray the Lords' Prayer
Mt 6: 9-13 (KJV)

Our Father which art in heaven, Hallowed be thy name.
Thy kingdom come, Thy will be done in earth,
as it is in heaven.
Give us this day our daily bread.
And forgive us our debts, as we forgive our debtors.
And lead us not into temptation, but deliver us from evil:
For thine is the kingdom, and the power,
and the glory, forever.
Amen.

Psalm for Prayer: Psalm 90

Going Deeper:

- Listen Long and Listen Hard. Lean into what the Lord is saying to you.
- Write it down. If the God of the Universe speaks to you, you might want to write it down.
- Hold it, turn it, and chew it.
- Act on it. Celebrate, Repent, Change.
- Share it.

Notes:

Three Day Landing

What is the three day landing?

In the Gospels we see that Jesus was big on celebrating with his disciples. Each time they were sent out, he would ask them to come back to share testimonies, to encourage one another, to debrief and to set a plan to keep moving forward. During our three day landing we will do the same. We will go deeper into the conversation of becoming more like Jesus, listen to testimonies, celebrate, probably cry a bit, and then plan for the next phase of obedience.

Session 1: Sympathetic Resonance Tuned to Eternity

A lesson in listening

What is the basis of our faith?

The Christian life consists in what God does for us, not what we do for God . . . the Christian life consists in what God says to us, not what we say about God. We also, of course, do things and say things, but if we do not return to Square One each time we act, each time we speak, beginning from God and God's word, we will soon be fond of practicing a spirituality that has little to do or nothing to do with God.

And so if we are going truly to live a Christian life and not just use the word 'Christian' to disguise our narcissistic and Promethean attempts at a spirituality without worshipping God and without being addressed by God, it is necessary to return to Square One and adore God and listen to God. Given our sin-damaged memories that render us vulnerable to every latest edition of journalistic spirituality, daily reorientation in the truth revealed in Jesus attested in Scripture is required. And given our ancient predisposition for reducing every scrap of divine revelation that we come across to a piece of moral/ spiritual technology that we can use to get on in the world, and eventually to get on with God, we have proven time and time again that we are not to be trusted in these matters. We need to return to Square One for a fresh start as often as every morning, noon and night.[4]

---

[4] Wrigley-Carr, Robyn, *Evelyn Underhill's Prayer Book*. SPCK Publishing, 2018

Notes:

Notes:

Session 2: Making Space for Grace

We are not attempting to earn
the love of God, He cannot love us any
more or any less, but we are attempting
to make space for grace.

The On-Ramps that Lead to an Exponential Life.

1. Listening
2. Asking (Prayer)
3. Wilderness
4. Community
5. Self-denial (Fasting)
6. Sabbath
7. Generosity
8. Beholding

Notes:

Notes:

Session 3: What Jesus Really Said

"The Christian does not think God will love us because we are good, but that God will make us good because He loves us."
-CS Lewis

"Nothing binds me to my Lord like a strong belief in His changeless love."
-Charles H. Spurgeon

"To know God's love is indeed heaven on earth."-J. I. Packer

Notes:

Notes:

Session 4: Growing, Permeating and Treasured

Matthew 13 (NLT)
Parables of the Mustard Seed, Yeast, and the Pearl of Great Price

31 Here is another illustration Jesus used: "The Kingdom of Heaven is like a mustard seed planted in a field. 32 It is the smallest of all seeds, but it becomes the largest of garden plants; it grows into a tree, and birds come and make nests in its branches." 33 Jesus also used this illustration: "The Kingdom of Heaven is like the yeast a woman used in making bread. Even though she put only a little yeast in three measures of flour, it permeated every part of the dough."

44 "The Kingdom of Heaven is like a treasure that a man discovered hidden in a field. In his excitement, he hid it again and sold everything he owned to get enough money to buy the field. 45 "Again, the Kingdom of Heaven is like a merchant on the lookout for choice pearls. 46 When he discovered a pearl of great value, he sold everything he owned and bought it!

Notes:

Notes:

Quick Reference Guide

Guide to the Ninety-day Walk

Day1 Matthew 1 Psalm 1	**Day 16** Matthew 16 Psalm 16	**Day 31** Mark 3 Psalm 31	**Day 46** Lk. 1:41-80 Psalm 46	**Day 61** Luke 16 Psalm 61	**Day 76** John 7 Psalm 76
Day 2 Matthew 2 Psalm 2	**Day 17** Matthew 17 Psalm 17	**Day 32** Mark 4 Psalm 32	**Day 47** Luke 2 Psalm 47	**Day 62** Luke 17 Psalm 62	**Day 77** John 8 Psalm 77
Day 3 Matthew 3 Psalm 3	**Day 18** Matthew 18 Psalm 18	**Day 33** Mark 5 Psalm 33	**Day 48** Luke 3 Psalm 48	**Day 63** Luke 18 Psalm 63	**Day 78** John 9 Psalm78
Day 4 Matthew 4 Psalm 4	**Day 19** Matthew 19 Psalm 19	**Day 34** Mark 6 Psalm 34	**Day 49** Luke 4 Psalm 49	**Day 64** Luke 19 Psalm 64	**Day 79** John 10 Psalm 79
Day 5 Matthew 5 Psalm 5	**Day 20** Matthew 20 Psalm 20	**Day 35** Mark 7 Psalm 35	**Day 50** Luke 5 Psalm 50	**Day 65** Luke 20 Psalm 65	**Day 80** John 11 Psalm 80
Day 6 Matthew 6 Psalm 6	**Day 21** Matthew 21 Psalm 21	**Day 36** Mark 8 Psalm 36	**Day 51** Luke 6 Psalm 51	**Day 66** Luke 21 Psalm 66	**Day 81** John 12 Psalm 81
Day 7 Matthew 7 Psalm 7	**Day 22** Matthew 22 Psalm 22	**Day 37** Mark 9 Psalm 37	**Day 52** Luke 7 Psalm 52	**Day 67** Luke 22 Psalm 67	**Day 82** John 13 Psalm 82
Day 8 Matthew 8 Psalm 8	**Day 23** Matthew 23 Psalm 23	**Day 38** Mark 10 Psalm 38	**Day 53** Luke 8 Psalm 53	**Day 68** Luke 23 Psalm 68	**Day 83** John 14 Psalm 83
Day 9 Matthew 9 Psalm 9	**Day 24** Matthew 24 Psalm 24	**Day 39** Mark 11 Psalm 39	**Day 54** Luke 9 Psalm 54	**Day 69** Luke 24 Psalm 69	**Day 84** John 15 Psalm 84
Day 10 Matthew 10 Psalm 10	**Day 25** Matthew 25 Psalm 25	**Day 40** Mark 12 Psalm 40	**Day 55** Luke 10 Psalm 55	**Day 70** John 1 Psalm 70	**Day 85** John 16 Psalm 85
Day 11 Matthew 11 Psalm 11	**Day 26** Mat. 26 Psalm 26	**Day 41** Mark 13 Psalm 41	**Day 56** Luke 11 Psalm 56	**Day 71** John 2 Psalm 71	**Day 86** John 17 Psalm 86
Day 12 Matthew 12 Psalm 12	**Day 27** Matthew 27 Psalm 27	**Day 42** Mark 14 Psalm 42	**Day 57** Luke 12 Psalm 57	**Day 72** John 3 Psalm 72	**Day 87** John 18 Psalm 87
Day 13 Matthew 13 Psalm 13	**Day 28** Matthew 28 Psalm 28	**Day 43** Mark 15 Psalm 43	**Day 58** Luke 13 Psalm 58	**Day 73** John 4 Psalm 73	**Day 88** John 19 Psalm 88
Day 14 Matthew 14 Psalm 14	**Day 29** Mark 1 Psalm 29	**Day 44** Mark 16 Psalm 44	**Day 59** Luke 14 Psalm 59	**Day 74** John 5 Psalm 74	**Day 89** John 20 Psalm 89
Day 15 Matthew 15 Psalm 15	**Day 30** Mark 2 Psalm 30	**Day 45** Luke 1:1-40 Psalm 45	**Day 60** Luke 15 Psalm 60	**Day 75** John 6 Psalm 75	**Day 90** John 21 Psalm 90

Guide to the 2nd Lap of the Ninety-day Walk

Day1
Matthew 1
Psalm 91

Day 2
Matthew 2
Psalm 92

Day 3
Matthew 3
Psalm 93

Day 4
Matthew 4
Psalm 94

Day 5
Matthew 5
Psalm 95

Day 6
Matthew 6
Psalm 96

Day 7
Matthew 7
Psalm 97

Day 8
Matthew 8
Psalm 98

Day 9
Matthew 9
Psalm 99

Day 10
Matthew 10
Psalm 100

Day 11
Matthew 11
Psalm 101

Day 12
Matthew 12
Psalm 102

Day 13
Matthew 13
Psalm 103

Day 14
Matthew 14
Psalm 104:1-18

Day 15
Matthew 15
Psalm 104:19-35

Day 16
Matthew 16
Psalm 105:1-25

Day 17
Matthew 17
Psalm 105:26-45

Day 18
Matthew 18
Psalm 106:1-23

Day 19
Matthew 19
Psalm 106:24-48

Day 20
Matthew 20
Psalm 107:1-22

Day 21
Matthew 21
Psalm 107:23-43

Day 22
Matthew 22
Psalm 108

Day 23
Matthew 23
Psalm 109

Day 24
Matthew 24
Psalm 110

Day 25
Matthew 25
Psalm 111

Day 26
Mat. 26
Psalm 112

Day 27
Matthew 27
Psalm 113

Day 28
Matthew 28
Psalm 114

Day 29
Mark 1
Psalm 115

Day 30
Mark 2
Psalm 116

Day 31
Mark 3
Psalm 117

Day 32
Mark 4
Psalm 118:1-14

Day 33
Mark 5
Psalm 118:15-29

Day 34
Mark 6
Psalm 119:1-8

Day 35
Mark 7
Psalm 119:9-16

Day 36
Mark 8
Psalm 119:17-24

Day 37
Mark 9
Psalm 119:25-32

Day 38
Mark 10
Psalm 119:33-40

Day 39
Mark 11
Psalm 119:41-48

Day 40
Mark 12
Psalm 119:49-56

Day 41
Mark 13
Psalm 119:57-64

Day 42
Mark 14
Psalm 119:65-72

Day 43
Mark 15
Psalm 119:73-80

Day 44
Mark 16
Psalm 119:81-88

Day 45
Luke 1:1-40
Psalm 119:89-96

Day 46
Lk. 1:41-80
Psalm 119:97-104

Day 47
Luke 2
Psalm 119:105-112

Day 48
Luke 3
Psalm 119a:113-120
Psalm119:121-12

Day 49
Luke 4
Psalm 119:121-128

Day 50
Luke 5
Psalm 119:129-136

Day 51
Luke 6
Psalm 119:137-144

Day 52
Luke 7
Psalm 119:145-152

Day 53
Luke 8
Psalm 119:153-160

Day 54
Luke 9
Psalm 119:161-168

Day 55
Luke 10
Psalm 119:169-176

Day 56
Luke 11
Psalm 120

Day 57
Luke 12
Psalm 121

Day 58
Luke 13
Psalm 122

Day 59
Luke 14
Psalm 123

Day 60
Luke 15
Psalm 124

Day 61
Luke 16
Psalm 125

Day 62
Luke 17
Psalm 126

Day 63
Luke 18
Psalm 127

Day 64
Luke 19
Psalm 128

Day 65
Luke 20
Psalm 129

Day 66
Luke 21
Psalm 130

Day 67
Luke 22
Psalm 131

Day 68
Luke 23
Psalm 132

Day 69
Luke 24
Psalm 133

Day 70
John 1
Psalm 134

Day 71
John 2
Psalm 135:1-12

Day 72
John 3
Psalm 135:13-21

Day 73
John 4
Psalm 136

Day 74
John 5
Psalm 137

Day 75
John 6
Psalm 138

Day 76
John 7
Psalm 139:1-12

Day 77
John 8
Psalm 139:13-24

Day 78
John 9
Psalm 140

Day 79
John 10
Psalm 141

Day 80
John 11
Psalm 142

Day 81
John 12
Psalm 143:1-6

Day 82
John 13
Psalm 143:7-12

Day 83
John 14
Psalm 144

Day 84
John 15
Psalm 145

Day 85
John 16
Psalm 146

Day 86
John 17
Psalm 147:1-9

Day 87
John 18
Psalm 147:10-20

Day 88
John 19
Psalm 148

Day 89
John 20
Psalm 149

Day 90
John 21
Psalm 150

Lord's Prayer
3Ninety3

"Our Father who art in heaven..."
There is a God and I am not him. He has a unique point of view
and knows the beginning from the end.

"...Hallowed be thy Name."
Pause until that first part sinks in.

"Thy kingdom come. Thy will be done,
On earth as it is in heaven."
He has a plan that I need to attempt to line up with. "There are two
kinds of people: those who say to God "Thy will be done" and those to
whom God says, "All right, then, have it your way" CS Lewis

"Give us this day our daily bread."
Wants Vs. Needs. "God does not give us everything we want,
but He does fulfill His promises, leading us along the
best and straightest paths to Himself." Bonhoeffer

"And forgive us our trespasses,
As we forgive those who trespass against us."
Refuse to let it build up. "Forgive, forget. Bear with the faults of others
as you would have them bear with yours. Be patient and understanding.
Life is too short to be vengeful or malicious." Phillips Brooks

"And lead us not into temptation, But deliver us from evil."
God will lead and deliver those who follow his path. "Faith never
knows where it is being led, but it loves and knows the One who is
leading." Oswald Chambers

"For thine is the kingdom, and the power,
and the glory, for ever and ever."
It's all yours and it's all under your control.
The outcomes are all yours and so is the glory.

"Amen."
So be it. "Faith takes God without any ifs. If God says anything,
faith says, "I believe it"; faith says, "Amen" to it." DL Moody

Take your journey deeper:

Join us as we reach back, lean in, and seek
out a deeper experience with God.
Go deeper with your host Joil Marbut at
Sage Spirituality Podcast.

SAGE *Spirituality*

JOIL A MARBUT

Learn more about this journey
in the book by Joil A. Marbut:

The Exponential Life

fscpublishing.com

Made in the USA
Columbia, SC
14 April 2024

34388071R00128